"The Weight of Money"

A Spiritual Journey

By Diane K. Leslie-Miller

401 Higganum Rd
Durham
(860) 575-6015
May 8 - 9th

Dedication

This book is a love letter to the Lord and His people and those that don't know Him yet. It represents the faith works that the Lord has ordained for me. Since 2003, He appointed my heart, in lieu of my will for teaching, counseling and freeing people from the idolatry and power of money. The purpose being, to unravel the message of love in HIS gospel.

This book is dedicated to my spiritual leaders and teachers, Pastor[s] Peter Leal, Sr. and Debbie Leal; to my supportive husband and spiritual covering, Daniel H Miller; and to Howard Dayton who introduced these teachings to me through his powerful ministry, and my three sons who inspired me every day to become a better mother, role model and teacher, Dustin, Jacob and Gabriel.

A special dedication to my son, Gabriel Nathan Miller, who went home to be with the Lord on November 19th, 2013, who displayed such an 'out-loud' passion for life and people that he truly taught me how to dismiss any fear and live according to the riches of an ordained life in Jesus Christ.

Table of Contents

Acknowledgments

Primarily, I would like to thank all the Aarons' and Hurs' that held up my arms, and encouraged me to deliver on God's prophetic word planted in my heart in 2009. Alike Moses, I have been commissioned, not necessarily qualified, to answer the call that has penned the strategy and vision with this ministry. When I had to take a very different direction in October 2017 it struck me solidly that God's plan is sometimes confusing, but never chaotic. Being a very disciplined 'ducks in a row' gal, I have had to learn to take the disappointments, delays, detours and mishaps with 'learned' flexibility. However, every leader needs a support team that is rallying, encouraging, contributing, praying and most of all, being there in the challenging seasons of doubt, fear and the world of 'what ifs'.

Therefore, I want to thank personally those saints in Christ that continually supported me in this new journey to see this book to print   Both Dan and I want to personally thank **Luz Reyes** for her wisdom, dedicated servanthood, and the rich friendship over the last 14 years; I would also like to extend a special thanks to **Frank and Jutta Frazier** who supported this ministry and vision for many of the early years serving faithfully, joyfully and whose cheerful contribution rallied us on. **Joe and Stella Gates**, who have been so faithful in their service to this Bible class and dear friends who shared our darkest hours; **Alshun & Melaida Stuckey** for their commitment in tearful prayers and strong belief in the value of this Bible study; **Donna Mamangan**, who has taught faithfully and possesses such a heart for sharing her testimony and experiences in life; **Kate Krupiczka** who has such a mature perspective and approach to God's word about financial stewardship and took immediate action becoming a living testimony of the blessings of doing life His way; **Anthony Scuito**, who has tackled this ministry full force and aided in many technical facets of getting this new class launched; **Evelyn Dudley**, who has taught at ease imparting her wisdom and life's experiences to bring the material to applicable knowledge for others; **Lillian and Dennis Kosswig**, who has been a delight over the last few years assisting us to teach this class with their seasoned wisdom; **John and Shannon Hebert**, a new addition to our team , but whose solid knowledge of the scriptures have made them an great asset to the class; **Marissa Meade**, who has been able to split her busy life of fashion world blogging and facilitate when she is not traveling to some exotic country. . And last, but not least, my dear **sweet husband** of 34 years, **Dan**, who has burned the midnight oil with me, served me tea faithfully while I am glued to the keyboard, who made me take a break every so often to breathe and enjoy life while I worked on this labor of love, and whose righteous prayers availed much to download revelation from the Lord. He will always amaze me with his profound Godly wisdom, perspective and calming spirit to balance out my tendency to 'heavy foot' life.

The Bible states clearly that the only debt we should ever take on is that of 'love' and I realized more than ever during this project that I am loved immensely through the hearts of other saints that I call my friends. God Bless you all richly for believing 'out-loud' through your actions

1) Keep me as the apple of your eyes

1   Identity Theft

Understanding who you truly are as a child of God starts painting a different perspective on how to live life. This will give you a new lens to view your daily comings and goings, not just in the external natural senses and abilities but much deeper with your spiritual gifts. When you truly understand and acknowledge how the Lord has created you for a special ordained purpose, you will start a supernatural journey that will be satisfying, successful and filled with contentment regardless of circumstances.

Study Scriptures:

(1) Psalm 17:8 & Proverbs 7:2 – I am the Lord's _____eyes_____ . *apple of his* *focus of the Lord.*

(2) Romans 12:4-8 & John 15:16; Eph. 2:10 – I am given __gifts__ to _use in our_ . *ministering*

(3) Ephesians 1:7; Romans 8:1; Hebrews 8:12 – I am _redeem and forgiven though his blood_ and free from __sin__ .

(4) Galatians 4:6-7; Romans 8:16-17; 1 Peter 2:9– I am a Child, SON of God's and therefore, share in His __heir of God through Christ__ .

(5) Philippians 3:13; Luke 9:62 – I will forget my __pass__ and not __look back__ .

(6) Romans 8:37-38; 2 Corinthians 4:6-12 – I am more than a __Conquerors__ in Christ that cannot be separated from His love and vessels of His __Love__ .

(7) 2 Corinthians 5:17; John 3:3-6- I am a New __Creation__ and given the Helper, the __Holy__ __Spirit__ being born again.

(8) Ephesians 1:3; Ephesians 2:3-5, 8; John 10:9 - I am spiritually __blessing__ and by His __grace__ , and believing the only _____ is through a personal relationship with Jesus Christ, am saved.

(9) 2 Cor. 5:20-21; Eph.f 4:24 – I am an __ambassador__ of Christ_ and represent the _____ of God. *true righteousness and holiness.*

I

(10)   1 Chron. 29:11-12; Ps 135:5-7; – I belong to the Lord because

He _owns_ and controls everything but my _free will_.

(11)   List three positive/encouraging statements that you can claim in Christ about your identity.
   * I am saved by faith
   * I am a son of God
   * God cleaned me of all my sins

(12)   Describe the difference between submission and/or surrendering to that of obedience.   to submit under the authority or power.

When you rely on God to work things out instead of trying to manipulate

(13)   Write a promise to your Savior as a covenantal promise from this day forward of living a life for Him.

Come to church every week because I always find things to do.

(14)   List what you are willing to give up to Him as part of this covenant. What is the hardest challenge to give up? Why?

time   money   ?

Assessment Exercises to Do

1. Spiritual Gifts Assessment:
Go to the following Links & Take the Test which is offered in several languages also…. English, Spanish, French, …etc:
http://www.spiritualgiftstest.com/test/adult [adult]
http://www.spiritualgiftstest.com/test/youth [youth]

To understand your Spiritual Gifts as a "Born-Again" Believer, go to the following Link:
http://www.spiritualgiftstest.com/faqs

Invest
Artistic
Real

IAR
AI
AIR

2. Talents/Natural Abilities Assessment:
https://www.123test.com/career-test/ [Free Career Test & others]

www.assessment.com [MAPP Assessment Method-Free Basic Test- Thorough Other Reports that charge a fee]

Goals to Set - Future Plans – Luke 14:28-30 & Prov. 24:27

List the plans you will do over the next week in preparing for your future . [Specific steps for education, job, business ideas , restoration with family, financial obligations, and spiritual growth] **Use your journal to list these.**

Sell my condo .

Post It Activity

360 Feedback. Hand out a Post-It note with one or more of the following questions to friends, family and/or business co-workers. [Try to get 5 if possible]
   1 – List a Character Strength/and or Skill I Possess?
   2 – What did you think about me when you first met me? [Brief sentence]
   3 - What do you think of me now that you know me well? [Brief sentence]
4 - What makes me different than others that you know?
5 - How do I come across in body language?

Let's Get Practical

How did your assessments change your perspective in what you are currently doing for a paycheck? Will you make changes, perhaps go back to school, gain a certificate or look for a different vocation? How did the "360" post it activity either confirm or surprise you on what others think about you?
Share your thoughts in your journal.

Identity Theft is not a casual problem in our society, so included is a link below where you can find interesting statistics, protective measures to minimize your risk, and the government agency that is following this rising problem.
   The Bureau of Justice Statistics department tracks 'financial identity theft' nationally. You can find these interesting statistics at the following link: https://www.bjs.gov/index.cfm?ty=tp&tid=42

Summary of Findings – 2014 –Report on Identify Theft

An estimated 17.6 million Americans—about7% of U.S. residents age 16 or older—were victims of identity theft in 2014. Most victims (86%) experienced the misuse of an existing credit card or bank account. About 4% of victims had their personal information activity stolen and used to open a new account or for other fraudulent activity. Some victims(7%) experienced multiple types of identity theft during the most recent incident. These findings were similar to those published in 2012.

Discovering identity theft

In 2014, an estimated 6 in 7 U.S. residents (85%) took actions to prevent identity theft; such as checking credit reports, shredding documents with personal information, and changing passwords on financial accounts. The majority of identity theft victims discovered the incident when their financial institution contacted them about suspicious activity (45%) or when they noticed fraudulent charges on their account (18%). Most identity theft victims did not know how the offender obtained their information, and almost all (9 in 10) did not know anything about the offender.

Victim characteristics

More females (9.2 million) were victims of identity theft than males (8.3 millions). Among racial groups, whites experienced identity theft at higher rates (8%) than blacks (5%), other races (6%), or Hispanics (5%). Victims ages 25 to 64 (8%) had the highest rate of identity theft, compared to all age groups. Persons in households with an annual income of $75,000 or more had the highest prevalence of identity theft (11%), compared to those in all other income brackets.

Financial loss

Two-thirds of identity theft victims reported a direct financial loss. Victims whose personal information was misused or who had a new account opened in their name experienced greater out-of-pocket financial losses than those who had an existing credit card or bank account compromised. About 14% of identity theft victims experienced an out-of-pocket loss of $1 or more. Of those ,about half suffered losses of less than $100 and 14% lost $1,000 or more.

Resolving identity theft problems

More than half (52%) of identity theft victims were able to resolve any problems associated with the incident in a day or less, while about 9% spent more than a month. Victims whose existing account was misused (54%) were more likely to resolve any financial or credit problems within 24 hours than victims of multiple types of identity theft (39%) or victims of new account fraud (36%). Fewer than 1 in 10 identity theft victims reported the incident to police. Victims who spent more time resolving the associated problems were more likely to experience problems with work and personal relationships and severe emotional distress than victims who resolved the problems relatively quickly. Among identity theft victims who spent 6 months or more resolving financial and credit problems due to the theft, 29% experienced severe emotional distress, compared to 4% who spent a day or less. Ten percent of identity theft victims reported that the crime was severely distressing, compared to 33% of violent crime victims.

Statistics can be found at **www.bjs.gov**. Source: Bureau of Justice Statistics, National Crime Victimization Survey, Identity Theft Supplement, 2012 and 2014.

There are many types of identity theft besides the common ones mentioned in this article. Go the following links to explore the various ways you can become a victim to your identity being stolen and how to protect yourself, report an event and protect yourself financially.

https://www.usa.gov/identity-theft#item-206115

https://www.identitytheft.gov/

✓ _You will want to immediately check your credit reports if you are compromised:_

https://www.consumer.ftc.gov/articles/0155-free-credit-reports

www.annualcreditreport.com   [This is the _ONLY_ web site you can receive a free credit report from all three credit bureau agencies; TransUnion, Equifax and Experian.
_Or_ call for your free credit reports @1-877-322-8228 /P.O. Box 105281, Atlanta, GA. 30348-5281

✓ Once you have your credit reports, you need to **obtain** your credit "score" known as your '**FICO**" **Score**, an accumulative average of your scores from each credit bureau. The base FICO® Scores range from **300-850**, and industry-specific FICO® Scores range from 250-900 higher is better.

FICO® Scores are calculated from many different pieces of credit data in your credit report. This data is grouped into five categories as outlined on the next page in the diagram. . The percentages in the chart reflect how important each of the categories is in determining how your FICO Scores are calculated.

Your FICO Scores consider both positive and negative information in your credit report. Late payments will lower your FICO Scores, but establishing or re-establishing a good track record of making payments on time will raise your score.

How a FICO Score breaks down

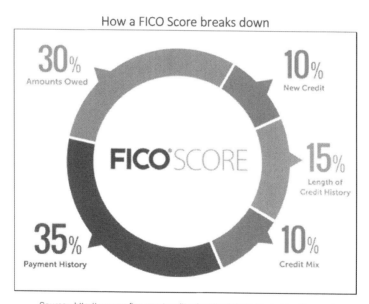

.Source: http://www.myfico.com/credit-education/whats-in-your-credit-score/

The website: **www.myfico.com** has great information all about your credit scores and what it means to you as a borrower Check out the calculators and education page to find out how long it will take to pay off a credit card at a particular interest rate, saving for child's education, types of mortgages and a wealth of other subjects for the consumer.
http://www.myfico.com/credit-education/calculators/

✓ <u>There are four main ways to get a credit score:</u>

1. **Check your credit card or other loan statement.** Many major credit card companies and some auto loan companies have begun to provide credit scores for all their customers on a monthly basis. The score is usually listed on your monthly statement, or can be found by logging in to your account online.

2. **Talk to a non-profit counselor.** Non-profit credit counselors and HUD-approved housing counselors can often provide you with a free credit report and score and help you review them.

3. **Use a credit score service.** Many services and websites advertise a "free credit score." Some sites may be funded through advertising and not charge a fee. Other sites may require that you sign up for a credit monitoring service with a monthly subscription fee in order to get your "free" score. These services are often advertised as "free" trials, but if you don't cancel within the specified period (often as short as one week), you could be on the hook for a monthly fee. Before you sign up to try one of these services, be sure you know what you are signing up for and how much it really costs.

4. **Buy a score.** You can buy a score directly from the credit reporting companies. You can buy your FICO credit score at myfico.com. Other services may also offer scores for purchase. If you decide to purchase a credit score, you are not required to purchase credit protection, identity theft monitoring, or other services that may be offered at the same time.

What does this involves?

Identity theft in the natural, someone's identity is stolen every two seconds. It is one of the fastest growing crimes in the United States. Someone steals information about you and then uses it to pretend to be you and take what is yours! Massive charges begin showing up on your credit card. Money disappears from your bank account. You are left with a mess that is difficult to correct.

Identity Theft – Don't Be a Victim

Spiritually there's a more devastating identity theft happening every second of every day. Tens of thousands of believers are having their identity in Christ stolen. To have your bank account ripped off is one thing but, to be robbed of your riches in Christ is a whole other story. You're a winner! 1 John 5:4 tells us, "*for whoever is born of God overcomes the world. And this is the victory that has overcome the world—our faith*." In other words if you are born again, if you've put your faith in Christ, you are born to win. It's part of your identity in Christ. It's who you are. Your identity is important. You need to treasure it and protect it. There is a thief that wants to still your identity! Don't become a victim of identity theft.

Beware of the Thief

El ladrón viene para matar, hurtar y destruir.

Jesus warns us in John 10:10. "*The thief comes only to steal and kill and destroy…*". The thief is the devil and he wants to steal from you. He wants to steal the truth of who you are in Christ. He will lie to you and deceive you to try to convince you that your a loser. He wants to take away your peace and joy by bringing thoughts of condemnation and guilt. The "thief" wants to steal your true identity by defeating you, discouraging you, robbing you of your privileges. and stopping you from living out your purpose and destiny. What should you do?

Guard Your Heart and Mind

You must take steps to guard your heart and mind. Proverbs 4:23 instructs us to, "*Above all else guard our heart, for out of it flow the issues of life.*" Proverbs 23:7 tells us, "*As a man thinks in his heart so is he.*" It is in your heart and mind you store the treasures of God's truth and out of that flows life. The New Testament over and over teaches us and reminds us of who we are NOW that we are in Christ. We are the elect, holy, and beloved (Col. 3:12). We are new creations old things have passed away (2 Cor. 5:17). We are joint heirs with Christ. (Romans 8:17) We are adopted sons, and daughters of God (Rom. 8:15-16). We are redeemed, and forgiven (Eph. 1:7). We are citizens of the kingdom of heaven (Phil. 3:20). We ARE complete in Christ (Col. 2:8-10). We are righteous. (2 Cor. 5:21). These are the realities – the truths of who we are in Christ. It is our identity. These truths need to be hidden in our hearts and they need to be what we think about. It is these truths that the enemy wants to steal because they are what make up your real identity.

It is imperative that you guard these truths by keeping your mind focused on them and not allow the lies and deceptions of the enemy to steal them. You must see yourself as God sees see you in Christ. You must accept yourselves for who God says you are. You must not let feelings, circumstances, or other people's opinions of you shape or define who you are. Guard your heart and mind to protect the truth.

Take Back What the Devil has Stolen

If you have experienced spiritual identity theft and have lost your confidence in who you are in Christ, it is time to take back what the devil has stolen. Jesus gave His life to give you a new identity. Take back your identity by remembering who He has made you. Declare God's Word over your life. Don't allow others label you. You are a new creation in Christ. *"old things have passed away; behold, all things have become new."* (2 Corinthians 5:17) Jesus promises us that the truth will set us free. You belong to Him. You are valuable. Don't believe the lies of the enemy. Believe the truth.

You Are Valuable Because

If I offered to give you a $100 bill would you take it? Absolutely, who wouldn't take a $100. Why? It's worth one hundred dollars. But, what if I crumbled it up, spit on, stepped on, rubbed it in the dirt, would you still want it? Sure you would. Why? It's still worth one hundred dollars. None of what I did to it changed its value. The value is based on the fact the United States government made it and stands behind it no matter how worn, creased, or dirty it is. So, it is with you. Your value is not based on what has happened to you in life or what you've done or not done. You are valuable because of who made you. Ephesians 2:10 tells us, *"We are God's workmanship"* Psalms 139:13 says you've been, *"fearfully and wonderfully made"* by God. You've been created "in the image of God" (Genesis 1:27) AND- He proved how valuable you are by how much He paid for you. He paid the ultimate price – He gave His life for you. You are valuable – priceless regardless of how messed up, dirty, or marred you may be. God stands behind you and with you. He will never leave you or forsake you! When you look in the mirror, who do you see? What do you see?

Make sure you see who Christ says your are – that is your true identity.

"Identity theft" – take steps today to stop the enemy from stealing your identity.

[*Source: http://breakthroughforyou.com/identity-theft/ Pastor Bruce Edwards · May 17, 2016]

2 Where Am I?

Oftentimes, when we think we are in a total crisis with our personal finances, it is what *we don't know* that kills us. So, it is critical to evaluate and assess your current situation on paper. So, this chapter we will define some basic assessment financial terms so you can manage your money and resources effectively, instead of your money managing your life's choices. But first let's dive into some scriptures to explore what God has attempted to teach His children from day "one" on the subject of stewardship and more importantly, trust.

Study Scriptures:

(1) Genesis 1: 26 -The Lord extended _____ to rule over all other living things and the earth.

(2) Genesis 2:15 – I am the Lord's_____wherever he places me to work.

Exodus 16:1-34 – After reading this entire story of what the Israelites had to be taught to become faithful in the Lord's provisions, answer the following questions:

(3) Verse 3: Even after the Israelites were removed from Bondage in Egypt, they complained to Moses about the lack of_____ and accused Moses that he brought them to the desert to _____.

  ❖ How does this echo with current times ? How does our media feed us with messages of entitlement?

(4) Verse 4: Lord told Moses that he would rain down bread from Heaven called_____ to _____ His children to see if they would _____.

(5) Verse 5: – The Lord provided a double portion on the sixth day? Why do you think He did this?

(6) Verses 6-8: Oftentimes, we alike the Israelites don't .think the Lord is listening to us in our lean, complaining, "why me", seasons. How does the Lord show His glory to the Israelites?

(7) Verses 9-11: Aaron gathered the Israelites to come before the Lord so they could _____ through Moses how their needs were going to be met. However, it would demand _____.

❖ How has the Lord tested your faith in a particular season of need?

(8) Verses 13- 15: The Lord was gracious to even supply Quail in addition, to the Manna. Why do you suppose the Lord supplied meat to the Israelites when they continually whined?

(9) Verses 16-19: List the specific instructions the Lord gave:

❖

❖ .

❖

(10) Verse 20: Some did not follow instructions from the Lord; what happened to their surplus food?

❖ Cite an example that you have purchased surplus food or other goods that went to waste. What did you learn?

❖ Think about purchasing items on credit, especially on "sale". Calculate what that item really cost you with interest added. What is the value of that item when it is completely paid.

❖ What emotions prompted the Israelites to disobey?

(11) Verses 21-30: Why was it important that the seventh day was kept holy for the Lord?

Why is this still a current practice for Believers today? {timeless truth of God's Word]

❖

What does Manna represent to you? [daily provisions, income, needs]

The "Trust" Factor

"It is Christ who is to be exalted, not our feelings. We will know Him by obedience, not by emotions. Our love will be shown by obedience, not by how good we feel about God at a given moment. "And love means following the commands of God." "Do you love Me?" Jesus asked Peter. "Feed My lambs." He was not asking, "How do you feel about Me?" for love is not a feeling. He was asking for action."
- Elisabeth Elliot,
Missionary & Wife to Jim Elliot, Ecuador

(12) <u>Verses 31-35</u>: Why do you think the Lord commanded the Israelites to take an omer of manna and place it in a jar before the Lord to be kept for future generations? [To remain obedient and to trust the Lord's providential care generationally; we must continue to keep teaching the power & glory of our Savior's precious promises & simple principles of stewardship] How can we model the 'jar of manna' lesson in our homes for our children?

(13) **Obey** – The Biblical word for "obey" comes from the Greek *"hupakou"* which means to listen attentively; by implication to heed or conform to a command or authority. This word conveys the idea of *actively* following a command. There is no choice in the matter, it is to be done whether one agrees with it or not. Obedience is involuntary.

Submit – The Biblical word "submit" comes from the Greek *"hupeiko"* which means to yield; to *passively* surrender to an authority. Submission is similar to obedience but in this case one might question what is being commanded. Submission is voluntary.

Explain your relationship with Jesus Christ, your Personal Savior, in terms of differences between obedience v. submission in your life. Cite examples where you obey and/or submit to your Savior and how you would explain this to a doubting Thomas in your life?

(14) <u>Read the following Scriptures</u>: James 1:22-25; Hebrews 11; Matt. 6:24; Rev. 2:4; Psalm 51 –

What common theme do all of these verses contain? How do you evaluate your faith walk?

[obedience is required, but with the right heart attitude of repentance]

❖

Alike Wedding vows, when you entered into a relationship with Christ, there are promises that you must protect, retain and mature over time. List several ways you are guaranteeing the relationship is healthy, thriving, growing and maturing.

❖

❖

The circle of the wedding band is also a symbol of **eternity**. The circle has no beginning or end and is, therefore, a symbol of infinity. Traditionally, the wedding ring is worn on the fourth finger of the left hand to protect and retain this devotion. This is because the vein in this finger was believed to lead directly to the wearer's heart.

Let's go over some simple measurements and terms about your financial health.

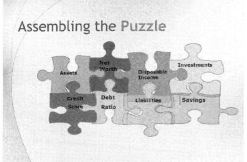

Assembling the Puzzle

(1) **Asset** – an item of value owned [minus any amount owed/fair market value]

(2) **Liability** - something (such as the payment of money) for which a person or business is legally responsible, normally debt owed to creditors.

(3) **Disposable Income** - income that is left after paying taxes and for things that are essential, such as food and housing. Normally used for investing, saving and/or luxury items.

(4) **Savings** - the excess of income over consumption expenditures [monthly expenses]

(5) **Investment** - the outlay of money usually for income or profit

(6) **Credit Score** - primarily based on credit report information, typically from one of the three major credit bureaus: Experian, TransUnion, and Equifax. ... FICO score, the most widely known type of credit score, is a credit score developed by FICO, previously known as Fair Isaac Corporation. Refer to Chapter 1 for more details.

Liabilities - What you owe

• What is an Liability?

Debt Ratio:

Calculation =

Total Monthly Debt payments / Total Monthly Income

Your debt-to-income ratio

- **36% or less:** This is a healthy debt load to carry for most people.
- **37%-42%:** Not bad, but start paring debt now before you get in real trouble.
- **43%-49%:** Financial difficulties are probably imminent unless you take immediate action.
- **50% or more:** Get professional help to aggressively reduce debt.

(7) **Debt Ratio** – How creditors calculate your debt-to-income ratio. This gives them a risk 'score' on whether you will be able to pay them back or not.

Calculation: Total Monthly Debt Payments divided by your Total Monthly Income [household].

Assessment: Calculate your Debt Ratio

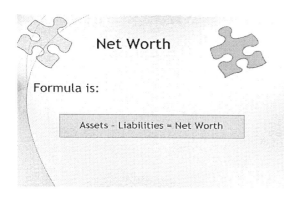

Net Worth

(8) Net Worth - refers to an individual's net economic position, the value of the individual's assets minus liabilities.

Formula is:

Assets - Liabilities = Net Worth

Assessment: <u>Calculate your Net Worth</u>

Goals to Set - Future Plans – Luke 14:28-30 & Prov. 24:27

<u>Create a Page in Your Journal named "My Net Worth in Christ" & Draw a Column for each subject below:</u>

1 – Own in Christ - What do you own becoming a born again believer in Christ?

2 – Owe in Christ - What do you owe becoming a born again believer in Christ?

➢ Try to list scriptures that support your 'net worth' in Christ

---

Post It Activity

➢ Write a Post-It note to rate where you are in your overall financial knowledge of managing your money [1 being the lowest to 10 being the most informed] & Why

➢ Write a Post-It note about the best advice that your parents gave you on money management

---

Let's Get Practical

To truly discover what is going on with the 'flow of cash' in your personal finances, you have to start tracking what money is coming in and in contrast, how much money is going out. Therefore, you must start implementing a method to record these transactions. Tracking for 30-90 days will give you a good idea on where your money is going.

<u>Here is a list of the top rated smart phone apps [most are free, but some have a small fee:</u>
PocketGuard , SpendBook, HomeBudget, Wally, Level Money, Spendee, YNAB, Mint, GoodBudget, Prosper Daily, Digit, Mvelopes and Expense IQ

If you are not a fan of smart phone apps, you can go to a search engine online [ie...Google] & find many free downloadable Budget Spreadsheets. Just be weary, because many 'debt consolidation counseling organizations' offer free worksheets but obtain your email address and/or phone number so they can solicit their services. [never free]

If you are not a computer savvy person or would rather do your tracking or budgeting with pencil and paper, well, you can go to any office supplies store, purchase a ledger and start tracking your income and expenses that method. Sounds old fashioned, but balancing your check book monthly really aids in discovering your spending habits and reoccurring expenses. And banks make mistakes frequently, so double check what is being taken out of your checking and saving accounts.

In this Study, we promote purchasing **"depreciating"** or "use" assets with cash to maximize negotiating power, and minimize value loss. You should avoid purchasing items on credit or via loans when they depreciate quickly. <u>Examples are:</u> vehicles, appliances, electronics, equipment and furniture. It is sometimes necessary to use credit wisely and purchase **'appreciating'** assets through loans, but again whatever you can afford in down-payments/deposits will lower you payment and maximize your cash flow. <u>Examples are:</u> property, houses, and investments like collections. It is always preferred to pay as much with cash as possible, because debt assumes there will be tomorrow to repay it and often times that is not the case. Avoid your legacy as *"unpaid debt"* to your loved ones.

To Understand the Categories in Simple Terms, you Basically Have "3" Categories in your Budget:

Needs, Wants & Desires

Your **Needs** constitute those necessities in life to sustain a healthy livelihood such as housing, food, medical insurance, clothing and transportation.
Why?

- Housing - Everyone needs a roof over their head; whether you rent or elect to acquire a home through a mortgage. If you do find yourself in a 'homeless' situation , especially with children involved, contact the following telephone number to identify assistance in your area. Contact a <u>housing counseling agency</u> in your area or call **800-569-4287** or go to the following website https://hudexchange.info/housing-and-homeless-assistance/ <Or> https://portal.hud.gov/hudportal/HUD . Contacting HUD will put you in touch with local services and programs to help you obtain affordable housing and many are subsidized by the government depending on your situation. There are program to help you with your utilities like heat which can be found at **www.acf.hhs.gov/ocs/programs/liheap**. For first time home owners, you can seek some assistance at **888-995-HOPE™ (4673)** at **www.makinghomeaffordable.gov**
- Food - Simply put, everyone needs to eat not only to survive, but to maintain a healthy lifestyle. Again, there are programs offered by your local State agencies to help you feed yourself and your family if consequences have left you hungry. Tap into these programs as every tax payer donates into them for the better of many. **www.hhs.gov** or **www.benefits.gov** . Biblically speaking, as believers following Christ's model, we are to help those in need especially our immediate family members. Too many seniors are struggling because the family is not pitching in to help them. Pray about being a blessing to your aging parents or even grandparents. [Read 1 Timothy 5:8] Additionally, if you can assist your aging family members to obtain social programs that they may not realize exists, that would help them also.
- Medical Insurance - Medical insurance is absolutely an non-negotiable for people. With rising medical costs, you are placing yourself and family at risk for catastrophic financial disaster by

going without. Refer to the top ten reasons on next page for bankruptcy in America. One single episode of care could land you in financial distress for decades. Again, the government offers many subsidized programs that help those in need at **www.healthcare.gov** or 800-318-2596. **www.medicaid.gov** and **www.medicare.gov** and **www.va.benefits.gov** are government programs that all have qualifying limitations. See **Table 1-B** for statistical breakdown of bankruptcy due to medical expenses. If you find yourself struggling with obtaining medical insurance, seek counsel.

- **Clothing** - It would be advisable to wear clothing, so yes, this is an essential need. If you are struggling to purchase clothes, there are many great consignment shops offering discounted 'gently used' clothing, or seek hand me down clothing from friends or family [co-ops have been formed for this very reason in communities] or purchase clothes during sales [with cash, not on credit] to maximize your cash. There are also local charities that oftentimes give clothes to those in need.

- **Transportation** - Everyone who is employed needs adequate transportation to get to and from work, shop for groceries or other necessities, medical appointments or just to enjoy some fun with friends eating out or traveling. However, this doesn't warrant that you need a car to do so. America is in love with the automobile and therefore, list these as essential needs which is not true. There are many who don't own a car and still get around.

Exclusions:

- **Vehicle** - Many people don't have the money to purchase a car/or make payments monthly, so they elect to use the municipal transportation system like buses or trains; they walk or bicycle to work if they live close by their employment or they arrange for a 'share ride'. Society screams you need a vehicle , however, if you can't afford payments, insurance and the general maintenance expenses that a vehicle generates, then think about alternative ways to travel.

- **Cellular Phone:** This is controversial but this isn't necessarily a 'need' because of the expense to have a phone. If you have a regular 'land line telephone' they are much less expensive for a monthly fee.   If your job or job hunting activities require a cell phone, and you have a limited budget, you can go to many retailers and purchase a "Pay as you Go" cell phone which excludes a contract and you add minutes as you need them.

- **Internet Access:** Some might argue in this technologically advanced society in America we absolutely need Internet access in our homes. This is listed as an exclusion because you can go to public libraries or other facilities to gain access to the Internet. Although, this can be a nuance rather than logging in from the comfort of your home, this is a 'free' service offered that doesn't fall under need.

Ten Top Reasons People Claim Bankruptcy

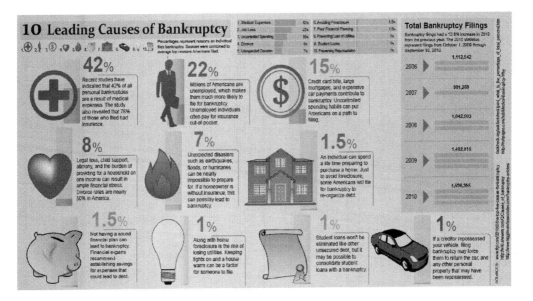

Statistics on filed bankruptcies in the U. S. as of 12/31/2016 were trending higher than a year previously.

TABLE 1-A

[Source:http://www.creditslips.org/creditslips/2017/01/bankruptcy-rate-rises-in-december-a-blip-and-not-a-blip.html]

Medical Bankruptcy by Age - Table 1-B

Age Range	% of Total Bankruptcies 2013, Estimated	US Medical-Related Bankruptcies 2013, Estimated	Size of Household	People Living in Households with medical-Related Bankruptcy 2013, Estimated
18-24	2.3%	14,618	2.41	35,229
25-34	18.7%	120,708	2.86	344,622
35-44	28.9%	186,812	3.35	624,888
45-54	26.4%	170,875	2.81	480,159
55-64	15.8%	102,080	2.18	222,534
65+	8.0%	51,719	1.76	90,767

[Source: NerdWallet Health Analysis]

Your **WANTS** constitute those things in life that are a step up from your essential NEEDS. Therefore, when you have established Biblical stewardship practices, and discover that you actually have disposal income [money left at your disposal to spend for non-essentials]

- A STEP up from NEEDS - - Some examples would be purchasing a car, or your first home after you save for down payments or deposits to lessen the payment or better yet to pay cash for those 'depreciating assets' and only extending credit for the larger 'appreciating assets'.

Your **DESIRES** constitute those things in life that are a step up from your WANTS. These items tend to fall into the luxury items, like boats, vacation homes, up-line vehicles, etc.

- A STEP up from WANTS - - These items should only be purchased when your disposal income is so extended that you are already meeting Biblical principles of Tithing, Saving and Investing already and still have surplus [extra] money. There is not a Biblical problem around wealth, which would fall into this category as long as you purpose it for the Lord's kingdom and glory.. [Read Luke 19: 11-27].

This Bible Study Promotes the - "70/30 Budget Method"

70%	Monthly Expenses: House, Transportation, Food, Clothing, Medical, Debts, Pets, Personal, Miscellaneous
10%	Tithing - Supporting your Home Church for Salaries, Building Costs, Equipment, Utilities, etc.
10%	Savings [Emergencies, Entertainment, Vacations, Replacement Assets, Planting Seed, Missions]
10%	Investments [Retirement Plans, Future Education, Missions, Planting Seed, First Fruits]

This Bible Study recommends the following break-down of expenditures:

Spending Categories	Includes	% of Total Income
70%		
Housing	Rent/Mortgage, Utilities, Property Tax, Insurance, Water, Septic, Gas/Oil, Maintenance, Grounds Upkeep	25-30%
Food	Groceries	5%
Clothing	Shoes, Formal, Informal, Necessities [socks, under garments, etc.]	5%
Transportation	Vehicles, Car Insurance, Buses, Trains	5-10%
Entertainment	Movies, Restaurants, trips, vacations,	5-10%
Medical & Health	Health insurance, medical expenses, pharmaceuticals, durable equipment, copays, coinsurance	10-15%
Non-Negotiables - To Establish Solid Biblical Principles		
30%		
Lord's Tithe	Expenses to cover home church expenses, including salaries of Pastor and staff	10-15%
Investments	Individual Retirement accounts, collectables, fine art, stocks, bonds, mutual funds, property [Appreciating Assets], Inventions, First Fruits, Missions, Seeds	10%
Savings	Start automatically withdrawing money to accumulate savings for emergencies, "use" asset replacements	10%

*Note: you can use whatever % you deem is more appropriate for your situation as long as it adds up 100%

The Gift of Forgiveness – Christmas Story

The Christmas of 1949 we didn't have a tree. My dad had as much pride as anybody, I suppose, so he wouldn't just say that we couldn't afford one.

When I mentioned it, my mother said that we weren't going to have one this year, that we couldn't afford one, and even if we could it was stupid to clutter up your house with a dead tree. I wanted a tree badly though, and I thought in my naive way that if we had one, everybody would feel better. About three days before Christmas, I was out collecting for my paper route. It was fairly late long after dark it was snowing and very cold. I went to the apartment building to try to catch a customer who hadn't paid me for nearly two months as she owed me seven dollars. Much to my surprise, she was home. She invited me in and not only did she pay me, she gave me a dollar tip! It was a windfall for me. I now had eight whole dollars.

What happened next was totally unplanned. On the way home, I walked past a Christmas tree lot and the idea hit me. The selection wasn't very good because it was so close to the holiday, but there was this one real nice tree. It had been a very expensive tree and no one had bought it; now it was so close to Christmas that the man was afraid no one would. He wanted ten dollars for it, but when I in my gullible innocence told him I only had eight, he said he might sell it for that. I really didn't want to spend the whole eight dollars on the tree, but it was so pretty that I finally agreed. I dragged it all the way home about a mile, I think and I tried hard not to damage it or break off any limbs. The snow helped to cushion it, and it was still in pretty good shape when I got home. You can't imagine how proud and excited I was. I propped it up against the railing on our front porch and went in. My heart was bursting as I announced that I had a surprise.

I got Mom and Dad to come to the front door and then I switched on the porch light. "Where did you get that tree?" my mother exclaimed. But it wasn't the kind of exclamation that indicates pleasure.

"I bought it up on Main Street. Isn't it just the most perfect tree you ever saw?" I said, trying to maintain my enthusiasm.

"Where did you get the money?" Her tone was accusing and it began to dawn on me that this wasn't going to turn out as I had planned.

"From my paper route." I explained about the customer who had paid me.

"And you spent the whole eight dollars on this tree?" she exclaimed.

She went into a tirade about how stupid it was to spend my money on a dumb tree that would be thrown out and burned in a few days. She told me how irresponsible I was and how I was just like my dad with all those foolish, romantic, noble notions about fairy tales and happy endings and that it was about time I grew up and learned some sense about the realities of life and how to take care of money and spend it on things that were needed and not on silly things. She said that I was going to end up in the poorhouse because I believe in stupid things like Christmas trees, things that didn't amount to anything.

I just stood there. My mother had never talked to me like that before and I couldn't believe what I was hearing. I felt awful and I began to cry. Finally, she reached out and snapped off the porch light.

"Leave it there." she said. "Leave that tree there till it rots, so every time we see it, we'll all be reminded of how stupid the men in this family are." Then she stormed up the stairs to her bedroom and we didn't see her until the next day.

Dad and I brought the tree in and we made a stand for it. He got out the box of ornaments and we decorated it as best as we could; but men aren't too good at things like that, and besides, it wasn't the same without mom. There were a few presents under it by Christmas day – although I can't remember a single one of them – but Mom wouldn't have anything to do with it. It was the worst Christmas I ever had.

Fast forward to today, Judi and I married in August of 1963, and dad died on October 10th of that year. Over the next eight years, we lived in many places. Mom sort of divided up the year – either living with my sister Jary or with us. In 1971 we were living in Wichita, Kansas. Lincoln was about seven, Brendan was three and Kristen was a baby. Mom was staying with us during the holidays. On Christmas Eve, I stayed up very late. I was totally alone with my thoughts, alternating between joy and melancholy, and I got to thinking about my paper route, that tree, what my mother had said to me and how Dad had tried to make things better. I heard a noise in the kitchen and discovered that it was mom. She couldn't sleep either and had gotten up to make herself a cup of hot tea – which was her remedy for just about everything. As she waited for the water to boil, she walked into the living room and discovered me there. She saw my open Bible and asked me what I was reading. When I told her, she asked if I would read it to her and I did.

When the kettle began to whistle, she went and made her tea. She came back, and we started to visit. I told her how happy I was that she was with us for Christmas and how I wished that Dad could have lived to see his grandchildren and to enjoy this time because he always loved Christmas so. It got very quiet for a moment and then she said, "Do you remember that time on Twelve Mile Road when you bought that tree with your paper route money?"

"Yes," I said. "I've just been thinking about it you know." She hesitated for a long moment, as though she were on the verge of something that was bottled up so deeply inside her soul that it might take surgery to get it out. Finally, great tears started down her face and she cried. "Oh, son, please forgive me." "That time and that Christmas have been a burden on my heart for twenty-five years. I wish your dad were here so I could tell him how sorry I am for what I said. Your dad was a good man and it hurts me to know that he went to his grave without ever hearing me say that I was sorry for that night. Nothing will ever make what I said right, but you need to know that your dad never did have any money sense (which was all too true). We were fighting all the time – though not in front of you – we were two months behind in our house payments, we had no money for groceries, your dad was talking about going back to Arkansas and that tree was the last straw. I took it all out on you. It doesn't make what I did right, but I hoped that someday, when you were older, you would understand. I've wanted to say something for ever so long and I'm so glad it's finally out."

Well, we both cried a little and held each other and I forgave her – it wasn't hard, you know. Then we talked for a long time, and I did understand: I saw what I had never seen and the bitterness and sadness that had gathered up in me for all those years gradually washed away. It was marvelously simple.

The great gifts of this season – or any season - can't be put under the tree; you can't wear them or eat them or drive them or play with them. We spend so much time on the lesser gifts – toys, sweaters, jewelry, the mint, anise and dill of Christmas – and so little on the great gifts – understanding, grace, peace and forgiveness. It's no wonder that the holiday leaves us empty, because when it's over, the only reminders we have are the dirty dishes and the January bills.

[Source: John William Smith – from "Hugs for the Holidays." Copyright ©1977 by Howard Publishing Co. Inc].

3   Ruler or Slave ?

The average American household has $132,086 in personal debt as of June 2016. This includes mortgages, credit cards, student, and car loans. All in all, the American people have $14 trillion in debt. That's an astonishing number, but it pales in comparison to the $19.5 trillion the government is in the hole. Individuals are recognizing the crippling effect of debt and we've seen recent trends of lower credit card balances from lower spending. So far, the government hasn't recognized what the people already know: when you're in a hole, stop digging. ※

Since the 2008 recession and the aftermath sent our economy reeling, Americans have shown great resilience in paying off some categories of debt and finding a secure financial footing. While credit card and other miscellaneous types of debt are on the decline, student and auto debt are both on the rise. Student loan debt has more than doubled nationwide in the past eight years.

Allowing Congress to overburden citizens with debt in the present means that our children and grandchildren will have to come to terms with paying off trillions of dollars in debt. Instead of putting money into projects that grow the economy (job creation, investments, and savings), future taxpaying adults face the risk of higher tax rates and a severe brake on economic growth.

[source: americansforprosperityfoundation.org]

To check out the national debt go to *http://www.usdebtclock.org/* and you can even select state level debt opposed to the entire United States; this is amazing how the debt clock is ticking away. As believers, we have a special stewardship to manage and minimize or eventually eliminate our personal debt. We have a choice to be camouflaged within our capital society or purposely choose to Biblically manage our finances against the "instant gratification", "fast food", "need it now" spending culture in which we live.

Read the "Word Study" and Answer the Following Questions:

1. .How do you view the payment that Christ has made on your behalf? *He died to pay for our sins.*

2. What if someone paid off all your financial debt? How would you repay them or would you? *I will always be grateful. I don't know if I would be able to pay back in the same way!*   *tetelestai*

Word **S**tudy:

"Tetelestai"

Literally translated the word *tetelestai* means, "It is finished." The word occurs in **John 19:28** and **19:30** and these are the only two places in the New Testament where it occurs. In **19:28** it is translated, "After this, when Jesus knew that all things were now **completed**, in order that the scripture might be fulfilled, he said, 'I thirst.'" Two verses later, he utters the word himself: "Then when he received the sour wine Jesus said, '**It is finished**,' and he bowed his head and gave up his spirit."

The word *tetelestai* was also written on business documents or receipts in New Testament times indicating that a bill had been **paid in full**. The Greek-English lexicon by Moulton and Milligan says this:

"Receipts are often introduced by the phrase [sic] *tetelestai*, usually written in an abbreviated manner..." The connection between receipts and what Christ accomplished would have been quite clear to John's Greek-speaking readership; it would be unmistakable that Jesus Christ had died to **pay for their sins.**

3. How does your life reflect the kind of gratitude worthy of Christ's redemptive 'paid in full'?

I follow his will, love him and love everyone else.

Study Scriptures:

(1) 1 Cor. 7:23 : - You were *bought* at a price; do not become *slave* to men.

(2) Gal. 5:1 : It is for freedom that Christ has set us free. Stand firm, then and do not let yourselves be *entangled* again by a yoke of *bondage*.

(3) Proverbs 22:7: ; Romans 13:8; Just as the *rich* rule the *poor*, so the borrower is servant to the *lender*. Do not any debt other than *love* for one another.

(4) Deut. 28: 15, 43-45 - What are the consequences of disobeying the Lord's commands? *course*
The alien who is among you shall rise and you shall come low.

(5) Deut 15:4-6; 28:1-2, 8-14 - What are the promises of obeying the Lord's commands?
The Lord will greatly bless you in the land which the Lord is giving you.

(6) Psalm 37:21: A Person is called *wicked* when they don't *pay* their debts.

(7) Proverbs 3:27-28: How you should repay your debts?
on time

(8) Proverbs 22:26-27; Proverbs 17:18; Proverbs 6:1-5: What do these verses instruct on co-signing?
Do not be one of those who shakes hand in a pledge.

(9) James 4:13-15: We Plan and God Laughs. Why is it presumptuous to purchase items on credit?
We do not know what will happen tomorrow.

(10) 2 Kings 4:1-7: Read the story of the Widow & the Oil & answer the following questions:

- What was the first thing the widow did? — *pray — ask for help*
She cried out to Elisha

- What did Elisha ask the widow ?
What she had in the house. He then asked her to go and borrow empty vessels

- Who helped the widow & her sons? Why?
Neighbors
God because she feared the Lord.

23

- How did the widow pay her debtors?

  By selling the oil

- How can we use the steps that the widow did to respond to financial crisis' in our lives?

  Pray, ask for help.

Let's Get Practical

✓ To understand the impact of purchasing things with credit cards or loans, you need to calculate the actual cost of an item when you are paying interest over time.

Exercise: Refer to the last big item you purchased [over $500.00] and calculate how much that item would really cost you if you finance it for 12 months at 10% interest? How much for 6 months at 25%? How much for 1 month @ 0% interest? [Add the original price to the interest over time to calculate total cost]

A couple of great web sites for all types of financial calculators can be found at: www.bankrate.com or http://www.calculator.net/finance-calculator.html or

➤ What happened to the value of that item? *It increase*
➤
➤ What has this taught you about your habit of purchasing items on credit? [if you do]
➤ *You will end up paying more.*

✓ What are your rights when your Debt Collectors Contact you?
Go to the following Link:
https://www.fdic.gov/consumers/assistance/protection/Debtcollection.html
<Or> https://www.consumer.ftc.gov/articles/0149-debt-collection
➤ What hours can debt collectors call you?

➤ What kind of practices are off limits for debt collectors?

✓ How do you feel when you can go purchase something? Think back to last time you experience buyer's remorse after purchasing something you couldn't really afford? Did you take the item back? Why or Why not?

➤ What choices are you eliminating when you have debt that minimizes your 'disposable income"?

- ✓ **Are you living paycheck to paycheck?** [According to a Survey in June 2016 at www.20Somethingfinance.com, 55% of the 25,000 people responding were living paycheck to paycheck, and would not be able to manage a $1,000 dollar unexpected expense without borrowing from friends, family or a lending institute. Yet another survey Bankrate published findings for in June of 2016 reported it like this…"More than 50% of Americans are one paycheck away from living on the street."

- ✓ Answer honestly - this will not be shared with the class. How much money do you have after your bills are paid?

- ✓ Do you have a savings account that you are accumulating at minimum $5,000.00 per year for emergencies?

- ✓ Have you established a Retirement Fund or any kind of Investment that you are growing?

- ✓ If you haven't been able to start your investment or savings accounts, find ways to cut monthly expenses, even if it a small amount? [Smart phone Apps: for Savings & Investing: : Acorns, Blooom, Robinhood, Betterment DIGIT] or meet with a Professional Financial Planner to help you navigate.

SHOW HIM the GRATITUDE by ACCOUNTABILITY

Top Ten Signs - Money is Managing Your Life

1. You are using credit cards to pay for necessities like groceries
2. You are paying just the minimum payment on credit cards
3. You have more than 3 credit cards that have double digit interest rates
4. You have to get another credit card because you have reached the credit limit on all others
5. You don't have any savings for emergencies
6. You haven't taken a vacation in over two years because you cannot afford one
7. You have not started any retirement or education savings/investments
8. If you lost your job, you could not pay your living expenses for 2 months
9. You have no idea how much money you spend every month
10. You want to tithe faithfully or give to missions, but you just don't have the money left

---

Some Proven Methods To Effectively "GET OUT OF DEBT"

(1) "First Things First" -- YOUR PART -"TO DO"

- ✓ Assess Your Situation - List out all Debt by Creditor, Interest Rates & Balances Owed. Work out a Plan of Repayment using one of the two methods outlined below and Contact your Creditors to execute on that Plan and then Stick to IT! There is a misquoted theory that has went around since 1950 from a plastic surgeon named Maxwell Maltz that a habit only takes 21 days to break. When in actuality it takes anywhere from 2-8 months. As Believers, we are to ask the Lord for any habits that block our full potential, so the Biblical Theory is that a habit takes just 1 day at a time to effectively change.

✓ Stop the Bleeding by Stopping the Charging & entertain a "slice and dice" party for your Credit Cards

✓ Liquidate unnecessary or surplus assets that could give you a jump start on paying off your debt. Your junk becomes someone else's treasures..

✓ Share your plan with friends & family to excuse yourself from gifts exchange for a 'set time period' to avoid further unplanned expenses. [unless you have an established savings plan reserved for gifts]

✓ Consider This - Every Spending Decision is a Spiritual Decision because you are either living within your means [what the Lord has supplied] or removing the Lord from those spending decisions and using a "plastic IDOL' to get what you want before you have what you need to get it. That is presumptuous. Get before the throne of the Lord and ask for help in your spending habits. Taking this class was the first step towards that by learning the 'truth' in HIS word.

(2) "FIRST THINGS FIRST" -- YOUR PART:"TO STOP" :

✓ Going into Denial on how bad your circumstances are by hiding from your creditors and ignoring their attempts at communications.

✓ Obtaining additional [new] Credit Cards or Loans to keep purchasing when you can't afford to pay your current debt

✓ Hiding this from your spouse and/or family that could help you face this issue; this can produce tremendous trust issues in your relationships

(3) "Snowball Effect Method" -Snowballing means listing all of your debts in order of smallest to highest dollar amount and then using any extra money to pay off the smallest

Account name			January 2012	February 2012	March 2012	April 2012	May 2012	June 2012
Lowes			$509	$0	$0	$0	$0	$0
Balance: $500	APR. 21%	Paid Off Date: Jan-12						
Student loan 4			$523	$484	$0	$0	$0	$0
Balance: $1,000	APR: 6%	Paid Off Date: Feb-12						
Student loan 5			$13	$562	$433	$0	$0	$0
Balance: $1,000	APR 4%	Paid Off Date: Mar-12						
Medical bill			$18	$18	$642	$348	$0	$0
Balance: $1,000	APR 9%	Paid Off Date: Apr-12						
Walmart			$37	$37	$36	$765	$579	$0
Balance: $1,350	APR 21%	Paid Off Date: May-12						

balance while only paying the minimums on the others. If you have a $10,000 student loan at 4% interest, a credit card balance of $17,000 with 17% interest, and a $23,000 car loan with 9% interest, you pay off the student loan first, followed by the credit card and finally the car. Once the smallest debt is paid, you move to the next smallest using the same strategy and include the amount you were paying on the first debt into your monthly payment on the next. You continue to do this until all of the debts are paid, the largest being last one to go. Why not pay the higher interest rate first? Psychologically, people need a 'win' on paying something off so this has been a proven success to start with your smallest debt.

(4) **"Stacking Method"** –To use the stacking method, you list your debts in order of highest to lowest interest rate, regardless of the dollar amount of the debt. You throw as much money as you can at the debt with the highest rate of interest. If you have the same debts we listed above, they would be ordered this way; the $17,000 credit card, the $23,000 car loan, and finally the $10,000 student loan. Once each debt is paid, you move down to the next highest interest rate one, again, using the money you were paying towards the last debt, and do the same. So on and so on until all the debts are paid. This method will save you in overall interest payments on your debt, however, it has been found to fail more because people don't experience success for a very long time.

Another Survey Showcases the Attitude of Most Folks when it Comes to Spending at the Holidays::
http://www.magnifymoney.com/blog/news/deeper-credit-card-debt-regrets-holiday

Survey Methodology: -The survey was conducted by Google Consumer Surveys for [www.MagnifyMoney.com] between December 24 – 26, 2015. 532 people responded to the questions in a nationwide, online survey. All respondents were 18 or older. The same trending for 2016 was expected.

✓ There was no spending plan or budget in place
- 50.7% *set no budget*. Instead, they "*just spent.*"
- 34.2% set a budget and followed the budget.
- 15.1% set a budget, but *ignored* the budget and spent more.

✓ A majority of Americans are "broke"
- 24.8% have less than $100 in their accounts.
- 23.8% have between $101 and $500 in their accounts.
- 7.7% have between $501 and $1,000 in their accounts.
- 16.4% have between $1,001 and $5,000 in their accounts.
- 27.3% have more than $5,000 in their accounts

** Most financial planners recommend having an emergency fund with at least $1,000. Ideally, the fund should cover three to six months of living expenses. 56.3% do not have even the minimum of $1,000.

✓ A significant minority will be paying off their credit cards for a long time
- • 61.7% of people will be able to pay their balance in full.
- • 27% will take some time, but pay more than the minimum due.
- • 11.3% can only afford to pay the minimum due

** For the 11.3% paying the minimum due, they can expect to stay in debt for more than **25 years** and will end up paying more interest than the original amount borrowed.

✓ **Despite the spending, we felt no regrets.**
- • 85.7% do *not regret* the amount of money they spent.
- • 14.3% do regret the amount they spent.
- • Of those with *no regrets*, 13.3% felt they could have *spent more*.

Lastly, **College Tuition Debt** - There is a myth that going to an Ivy League college or spending in excess of 40K per year for tuition will land you that six figure job. Statistics prove this isn't so and it is more about who you know that gets your foot in the door for most opportunities. Even advanced degrees doesn't really guarantee a higher salary.

There are a few rules you should follow if you are not sure how much debt you should take on when pursuing a college education:
✓ -**First**, your maximum *student loan debt* should not pass your expected annual salary after college.
✓ -**Second,** you should do your own market analysis of the field you are going into. Many of these schools promise unrealistic placement data.
✓ -**Third**, if unsure, look at 2-year state schools and transferring to a state 4-year institution. Because of budget constraints and the above factors, state schools have gotten more competitive because people realize the other options are either too expensive or simply not worth it.
✓ -**Finally,** If you really want to go to a private institution, consider a state school first and transferring into a graduate degree later.

The net worth gap between younger and <u>older Americans</u> is already large enough and doesn't need to be bigger with the saddling of <u>student debt</u>:

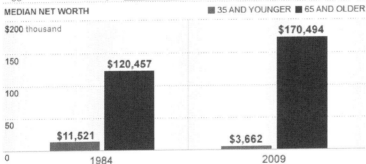

Source: CNN Money

To expect a 17 or 18 year old to understand this is hard to see but parents need to step it up but-with the average per worker salary being $25,000 it is doubtful many parents have the resources to run an in-depth market analysis when it comes to choosing the right school or program. As usual do your own due diligence and don't be fooled by the notion that all colleges are created equal and that college is priceless. At these cost levels, you better believe that there is a significant price. *[source: http://www.mybudget360.com/is-college-worth-it-money-and-debt-cost-of-college-and-student-loan-debt-for-profit-education/]*

If you still have Student Loans - Go to the following web site to see if you qualify for any of the
"forgiveness programs" https://studentloanhero.com/blog/the-complete-list-of-student-loan-forgiveness-programs/

Goals to Set - Living Within Your Means – Phil 4:12-13

As you pen some practical steps to get out of debt, remember your plans on how you will continue to work towards the 70/30 financial model outlined in Chapter Two. Jot down some thoughts on what it means to you to be content in any circumstance after reading the scripture above.. **Use your journal for this..**

Post It Activity

<u>Take a quick inventory in your house to Identify potential assets to sale:</u>
❖ Stick a Post-IT Note to any item that you could sale to raise some cash
❖ You can find fair market value for Vehicles at **www.kbb.com** [Kelly Blue Book]
❖ For collections or other items, you can research and find a fair market value on Online Auction Sites like **www.ebay.com**, Craig's List, or Social Media Sites like Facebook that have established Tag Sales dedicated to sell used assets like furniture, clothing, electronics, etc.

H ere's How Paying Off Debt Improves Your Happiness

Debt is a drag. Not only on your credit score, but also on your psyche. It's a dark cloud that lurks over many corners of life, casting a shadow over your confidence, ambitions and relationships.

The stress that comes from debt "may even completely eliminate all the happiness that you can get from spending your money," says Ryan Howell, associate professor of psychology at San Francisco State University and co-founder of Beyond the Purchase, a website that .examines the psychological link between money and happiness.

But a massive debt payoff can bring a host of psychological benefits. The achievement can restore your self-esteem and help you pursue life goals. The debt "pay-down" process instills a sense of resolve that will help you stay financially healthy. If that's not motivation enough, consider this: the trickle-down effect can lead to improved health and restored relationships, says Carole Stovall, a psychologist and executive adviser in Washington, D.C. When you're living with massive debt, it's easy to put your life on hold. All of those life dreams -- getting married, launching a business, having a baby -- seem impossible to pursue when your financial life is in disorder.

Hildebrandt and her husband could hardly fathom achieving her goal of purchasing a home with her 11 credit cards and a substantial personal loan, but after those grueling years of paying down their debt, they saw their credit scores rise and their finances stabilize. As they approached the "debt free" finish line, they closed on a house with a low fixed interest rate.

After clients pay off debt, "it gives them a lot more freedom," says Chris Dlugozima, community relations coordinator for Green Path Debt Solutions in New York. "I had a client (who) came in to see me; he was devastated. His fiancée had found out about his financial situation. He wasn't sure if the marriage was going to go through." Dlugozima worked with him to put him on a special payment program that helped him steadily knock off debt. Now, several years later, this client is not only married, but expecting twins.

"It's not just about the money, but about how the money can get in the way of life's other goals," says Dlugozima.

Confidence in your sense of self

The benefits of paying off debt go well beyond the bank. So whether you're nearing the finish line or miles away, think about these ways debt payment can help return balance to your mind and body. Less stress, improved health. It's no surprise that owing buckets of money puts a strain on life, but did you know that it's ranked as **one of the most stress inducing life events? "Getting into debt beyond means of repayment" is ranked No. 5 on the Society of Occupational Medicine's 2001 "Life Events Inventory," which ranks the psychosocial stress of 100 life events.**

The list ranks debt as more stressful than finding out your partner cheated on you. That stress takes a mighty toll on your body, says Stovall. "Stress is one of the drivers for health conditions related to cardiovascular disease, allergies, diabetes (and) gastrointestinal disorders," says Stovall. That's why paying off debt can result in physical healing. "When people pay off debt, they're going to say 'My stomach feels better, my heart feels better,'" says Stovall.

When Kandy Hildebrandt and her husband were paying off $122,000 of debt, the stress hurt the Wisconsin couple's health. Then they paid off their debt in four and a half years. The stress melted away. Balance has been restored to the family's finances, which Hildebrandt says is "awesome."

Emotional relief

Eliminating debt is more than just a numbers game. It's an act of breaking free from difficult past experiences. Debt associated with rough events -- such as divorce or a reckless phase in life -- is painful to carry around. So when you finally cut that debt from your life, you'll likely "experience tremendous emotional liberation," says Dallas-based financial adviser Derrick Kinney, who has seen this reaction especially in divorced clients. "Paying that debt off ... separates them from the other person," says Kinney. That enthusiasm can lead to better financial and personal decisions in the future. "They don't want to go back to what they experienced because the pain was so great," he says. For Hildebrandt, she associates those years of paying off debt with a very difficult time in life. She cared for their three children while her husband worked two jobs, his day job as a chemist and a night job mopping the floors of a grocery store. He barely slept. And when gas prices rose, he slept in his car overnight, even through the brutal Wisconsin winters. Once they were free from debt, he quit his part-time job. Now, when he walks into a grocery store, Hildebrandt says her husband always stops and looks at the floor. "He's relieved he doesn't have to do that anymore."

Freedom to pursue other life goals

When you're living with massive debt, it's easy to put your life on hold. All of those life dreams -- getting married, launching a business, having a baby -- seem impossible to pursue when your financial life is in disorder. Hildebrandt and her husband could hardly fathom achieving her goal of purchasing a home with her 11 credit cards and a substantial personal loan, but after those grueling years of paying down their debt, they saw their credit scores rise and their finances stabilize. As they approached the "debt free" finish line, they closed on a house with a low fixed interest rate.

"It's not just about the money, but about how the money can get in the way of life's other goals," says Dlugozima. Debt carries a huge stigma and can weaken self-esteem at its root. "Real financial stress -- it eats a person's soul in a way that's very different than other parts of our lives," says Howell. The shame associated with debt can drive people to mask their hardship in unhealthy ways. "You can still have the nice house, the nice things," says Dlugozima. "But really, behind it, the financial walls are crumbling." Indebtedness is painful, but so is losing face when it comes to light. "People are pretty unforgiving ... when you essentially lose financial trust," says Howell.

After Francine Bostick and her husband, a couple based in Kansas, paid off $120,000 of debt in five years, they could finally afford to buy a new car for the first time in their lives. "When (the car salesman) said they were going to run the credit check, I started to get that sick feeling, (like) when I had debt," says Bostick. "Then I thought, 'No, this is going to be good. Come on, run it!' I couldn't wait." Confidence turns on like the flip of a switch, Dlugozima says, adding that people even want to share their debt stories. "You become more open about it because you've gotten through the other side," says Dlugozima. "It's empowering."

The strength of mind to not return to debt

When you pay off a big debt, you strengthen your resolve to stay financially solvent. That comes with one important caveat: Your ability to stay out of debt likely depends on how you paid off your debt, says Kinney.

If you worked hard to steadily pay off your debt, you likely have practiced discipline to keep your finances in check going forward. "The clients that really push through over a number of years and a lot of sacrifice kept their debt paid down," Kinney says. Even though she's now "debt free", Hildebrandt's family has remained strict with their spending. "We just worked too hard to go back into debt," she says.

But this resolve may not stick with you if you paid that hefty tab with a windfall, such as a bonus or inheritance. "Down the road, (these) people are likely to go back into debt because they didn't earn the money and they didn't have any 'sweat equity' in paying off the debt," says Kinney. Of course, if pennies from heaven fall into your life, Dlugozima says it makes sense to put it toward your debt. "But if it's just done in a vacuum in a way where you're not looking at your spending or budget, you're doomed to repeat the sins of the past," he says. "The two need to be tied together to make it stick."

Improved relationships

The relief that comes from resolving financial difficulties has a generative power. A marriage that survived the challenge -- without the casualties of lost respect or bitterness -- will likely grow stronger, says Stovall. The process of paying off debt also encourages couples to communicate more honestly. Dlugozima says his organization frequently receives calls from people who want to fix big financial blunders before their spouse finds out. But for couples such as the Hildebrandts and the Bosticks, full disclosure allows partners to attack the problem -- not each other. **If a couple is functioning better, "that absolutely has a trickle-down effect on children,"** Stovall says. What's happening on a psychological level is a massive reduction of stress, making the parents less anxious or depressed. As Bostick drew near to paying off her debt, her adult daughter told her that "I was a lot nicer to be around. I wasn't as snappy."Kinney finds that **parents also become more vocal about teaching their children responsible financial behavior and sharing their success story with neighbors, friends and even strangers.** When Hildebrandt shared her story with a few publications, she received letters from folks who heard her story and were encouraged. "They said, 'What you did in four years is somebody's house!' One said, 'I don't have that much debt; I'm going to start paying off my mortgage sooner.'"

An Altered link between Spending and Happiness

Let's be honest. Spending money triggers emotions. It can feel good to buy those designer jeans, and it can feel great to anticipate the happiness those jeans will bring. This is what they call retail therapy. But debt payment is painful, and once you've felt that pain, the equation between money and happiness can change. Howell's research looks at the lasting emotional impact of different purchases. "People tend to expect that certain types purchases are going to make them a lot happier than they really will," he says. "It's not that they won't make them happy at all, but their bang for the buck is much smaller than they anticipate." Typical big bummers: electronic devices, clothing and video games, to name a few. Likely joy creators: experiences, such as dinner with friends or a weekend getaway. Back in the day when Bostick was sinking into debt, "I spent money on just getting stuff for my adult children and my grandchildren." It seemed important at the time, but climbing out of debt shifted her views on what's truly important. "Now it's like, you don't need to spend that money. They love you, whether it's a $5 gift or a $500 gift."

A New set of Temptations

After you put your last debt payment behind you, a new set of temptations will rush at you. For one, your restored credit score will flag credit card companies, who will try to woo you with competing offers, says Dlugozima. The moment a new card application pops into Hildebrandt's mailbox, "I immediately throw it in the garbage," she says. That kind of swift resistance is necessary to avoid the onslaught of temptations. Stovall says the newly "debt free" may feel enticed to celebrate their solvency by making a big purchase. But that's exactly the wrong move. **"Whatever they did to pay off debt is really the new normal,"** she says. Kinney **recommends small treats when quarterly or yearly goals** are achieved. It's important to celebrate success. "That way you're meeting the need to be rewarded along the process, and not building it up so you just want to go on a spending binge after you've paid off all your debt," he says. For Hildebrandt, **her biggest temptation "is to not delay gratification."** Once her family emerged from debt, she couldn't help but notice all the things they needed. But instead of purchasing everything that came to mind, they made a list, prioritized and bought only the most pressing items within their budget. **"Real financial stress -- it eats a person's soul in a way that's very different than other parts of our lives,"** says Howell. **The shame associated with debt can drive people to mask their hardship in unhealthy ways.** "You can still have the nice house, the nice things," says Dlugozima. **"But really, behind it, the financial walls are crumbling."** Indebtedness is painful, but so is losing face when it comes to light. **"People are pretty unforgiving ... when you essentially lose financial trust,"** says Howell.   { *Source: d. Lee, bankrate.com Sep. 3, 2013, 5:01 pm}*

4   Truth   or   Counsel-Quences?

In our society, it is getting tougher and tougher to believe anything that is communicated out of our politicians, leaders, employers, bosses, relatives and sometimes our children or spouses. However, as Christians, we are to operate at a higher level of integrity, always striving to be truthful with the shadow of grace guiding us. You can be truthful without being hurtful. Although, not to the point of blending into the political correctness model of today's culture in America; the belief that 'you're okay and I'm okay' and if people just leave each other's affairs alone, 'we will all be okay'. **Tolerance**. Just be *Tolerant* of one another.

"The frequent requiring and using of oaths, is a poor reflection on Christians, who should be of such acknowledged fidelity, as that their sober words should be as sacred as their solemn oaths."
- Matthew Henry

A recent interview [7/21/16] that Katie Couric did with the Neurosurgeon Ben Carson illustrated this new "watered down" term called "tolerance" regarding transgender freedom in defining their identity. Katie Couric *questioned* Mr. Ben Carson *"shouldn't we be exercising tolerance when he stated that you cannot change the biology or DNA of a female or male because of their feelings on who they think they are sexually?"* Ben responded with the following, *"Tolerance works in both directions...I believe the Constitution protects everyone with equal rights ... no one gets extra rights ... no one gets to redefine everything for everybody else and then make them comply to those ....that's not tolerance."*

Tolerance has a negative effect on many aspects of the spiritual life of a believer:

- It affects his **relationship** to Christ, who is Truth (John 14:6), and yet truth and tolerance cannot co-exist.
- It affects your **study** and understanding of God's Word, which is truth (John 17:17).
- It affects our ability to **love** because love rejoices with the truth   (1 Corinthians 13:6).
- It affects our ability to **worship**. Christ says, true worshippers shall worship the Father in spirit and truth; for such people the Father seeks to be His worshippers. God is spirit, and those who worship Him must worship in spirit and truth   (John 4:23-24).
- Finally, adherence to tolerance affects our **freedom**. Christ said, everyone who commits sin is the slave of sin (John 8:34). Not only is it right to adhere to truth, it produces freedom; If you abide in My word, then you are truly disciples of Mine; and you shall know the truth, and the truth shall make you free (John 8:31-32).
- After reading these verses, one might ask, Why would a believer practice or endorse such an unbiblical view which destroys **truth**? (Romans 2:8) reveals the answer. Those who do not obey the truth, Paul says, are selfishly ambitious.

Absolute Truth does not Compliment or Run with Tolerance

George Barna, in his book "What America Believes: An Annual Survey of Values and Religious Views in the United States" (p. 85), states: **"53% of Bible believing conservative Christian adults do not believe in absolute truth"**. The reason they *do not believe in absolute truth* is because they **do believe in tolerance**. If morality is independent and varies with the individual, then the possibility for justice and reason are lost. To those who accept tolerance and thereby reject truth, Charles Finney claims, "there is no reasoning with such a one" (Charles Finney, "Finney's Systematic Theology," p. 17).

[Source: Rebecca S. May www.relationalconcepts.org]

Honesty portrays the very nature of God. That promise is outlined in **Hebrew 6:17-19** that it is impossible for God to lie. This oath is a promise to every Christian to lay hold of the **anchor of hope** that we can undoubtedly trust Him in His *unchangeable nature*. As Believers, we should strive to emulate Christ's nature to progressively look and behave more like Him. And therefore, being honest with ourselves is the first step to being honest with others. Honesty is not "expressing everything that goes through your mind." That's transparency, and without a pause and an extra dose of His grace, that can lead to insensitivity or "finding the speck in someone else's eye". However, no one can be consistently honest without a **commitment to the truth**. Honesty will, at times, hurt someone's feelings, but that does not mean that *dishonesty* is preferable. Speaking in love with always buffer the delivery of necessary truth.

Speaking the truth in love requires that you have a **relationship** with a person more than a casual five minute conversation at Church on Sundays; it is quite senseless to think that someone will receive the truth if you haven't attempted to connect with that brother or sister to develop trust. If you think about what it has taken you to trust your Savior, as your Lord over your life, why shouldn't the same hold true in our earthly relationships. Get to know someone who you want to encourage in their challenges. And then say it in love truly desiring continual spiritual growth. Building relationships creates a Christian community that promotes growth, fellowship and a bond greater than anything else the world has to offer. It also creates a network of mentors, disciples, spiritual family members and friends whose counsel is priceless and distinct from the secular society.

Today' s Cultural Definition of "Tolerance" is "*Blanket Grace*", a Cheap Imitation of God's *True Grace*:

➢ In the two gospel accounts, Christ compares the sin of one group of people to the sin of another. With reference to His disciples, Christ says, *And whoever does not receive you, nor heed your words, as you go out of that house or that city, shake off the dust of your feet. Truly I say to you, it will be more **tolerable** for the land of Sodom and Gomorrah in the day of judgment, than for that city* (Matthew 10:14-15). The sin of both will not be tolerated. Actually, Christ is **describing His degree of intolerance**.

➢ With reference to the cities of Galilee, Christ says, *Woe to you, Chorazin! Woe to you, Bethsaida! For if the miracles had occurred in Tyre and Sidon which occurred in you, they would have repented long ago in sackcloth and ashes. Nevertheless I say to you that it shall be more **tolerable** for the land of Sodom in the day of judgment, than for you* (Matthew 11:20-24). In comparing the sin of one city to another, Christ, again, is not describing His tolerance of sin, rather He is **emphasizing His degree of intolerance**.

➢ **Revelation 2:19-20** is the only other place tolerance is mentioned in the Bible. In His message to the believers in Thyatira, Christ says, I know your deeds, and your love and faith and service and perseverance, and that your deeds of late are greater than at first. But I have this against you, that you tolerate the woman Jezebel, who calls herself a prophetess, and she teaches and leads My bond-servants astray, so that they commit acts of immorality and eat things sacrificed to idols *(Revelation 2:19-20)*. The Greek word which is translated "tolerate" in verse 20 is aphiemi, which means *"to send away, leave alone, or permit."* It is here where we can see exactly what is going on within Christianity today. Believers do good deeds, they love one another, they have faith and are growing in Christ. Yet *rather* than judge one another's sin, which is commanded *(Matthew 18:15-17)*, we tolerate sin. *Tolerance of sin is sin.* If Christ were to critique believers today, He might say, I have this against you, that you "send away" and/or "leave alone" sinners rather than confronting them in their sin. You permit sin for the cause of tolerance, thus endorsing the very thing you claim to hate. Rather, "these are the things which you should do: *speak the truth to one another*; judge with truth and ... let none of you devise evil in your heart ... and *do not love perjury; for all these are what I hate," declares the Lord* *(Zechariah 8:16-17)*.

Therefore, Tolerance for the Christian is:

> **Empathy** towards the condition of the human spirit and psyche that prompts us to reach the lost for a full redeemed life into His light

> **Grace** extended to save souls by means of evangelism, discipleship, teaching the truth...the "Word of God"

> Cannot contradict the Word of God; sin is sin

> **Judging** the sin, not the Sinner and by sharing the truth will set them free from the bondage of lies

> Should **Focus** on the purpose of **Salvation**

> IS not the same as GRACE

> Is a Deception from the Devil who is the father of all lies. [John 8: 43-44]

GRACE:

the free and unmerited favor of God, as manifested in the salvation of sinners and the bestowal of blessings.

http://www.biblestudytools.com/dictionary/grace/

GRACE for the Christian:

> Unearned favor from the Lord when you entered into a relationship with Jesus Christ as your Lord and Savior,

> A redemptive supernatural decision that allowed the Holy Spirit to give you a new spiritual birth [born again]

> Being under the covenant of His Love Letters to you [Holy Bible], you enter into a relationship to get to know His expectations of how you live your life by studying His Absolute truth, HIS Word

> Understanding that there is a different standard of integrity of character to become more Christ Like

> Obeying his commandments lead you on a 'narrow path' which in actuality gives you full liberties under His providential care

> That Love covers a multitude of Sin, and that love is God Himself [Trinity] and therefore, God is Truth, the one and only :"Absolute Truth". Therefore, Grace is not to be confused with Tolerance.

Study Scriptures:

(1) Psalm 116:11 -Humankind is not naturally _honest / Liars_ . .Prov. 17:4: Liars pays attention to _spiteful tongue_

(2) Rev. 21:8:: Liars will end up in the _lake of fire_ . Jer. 9:5: Alike our modern culture, everyone is _lying to one another_

(3) 1 John 2:21-22: A liar is defined as one who denies _Him_ as the _truth_ . And 1 John 2:4: A man who says I know Him but does not do what He _said_ is a liar.

(4) Eph 4:15: Speaking the truth in _love_ we are to grow up in every way. Prov. 27:6: _Wounds_ from a friend can be _deceitful / trusted_ but an enemy multiplies kisses.

(5) Heb. 6:18: It is impossible for God to _lie_

(6) Lev. 19:11-13: The Lord commands us to _not lie to one another_

(7) Deut. 25:13-16: The Lord commands us to be fair in our _business dealing_ .

(8) Prov. 12:15: Why should we listen to counsel? _to be wise_ Prov. 13:10: What is the consequence of not seeking counsel? _nothing comes but strife_

(9) Heb 4:12 & 2 Tim 3:16-17: Why should the Bible be a resource to you for problems in life? _discerner of the thoughts and intents of the heart_ .

(10) Prov. 1:1-3: What should you avoid in seeking counsel? _Sit amougt negative sinners! study Bible_ Note: Beware of the counsel that is biased that he or she could benefit from it.

(11) John 14:6: Jesus states " I am the _the: Truth_ and the Life. No one comes to the Father except through _Him_

37

(12) **Phil 2:15:** We must prove ourselves to be __*children* *of God*__ and above the reproach of the __*likeness of men*__ and perverse generation. Our lives are our living testimony; if we don't prove

trustworthy, how will be reach anyone?

Goals to Set - *The Condition of the Heart* — *Jer. 17:9*

Write about two experiences when (1) someone lied to you & (2) When you lied to someone. <u>Answer the following questions in an Two Columned Table :</u>

(1)   Was it someone you knew well or a casual acquaintance? Which hurt more?

(2)   How did it make you feel?

(3)   What prompted the lying? [To Hide, To Protect, To Cover] both sides

(4)   Did these events make it easier or harder to continue to lie? Why?

What will you do in the future to avoid, or stop the lying? [both sides]

Use your Journal to record these thoughts

Post It Activity

<u>Take a quick inventory for the next week on lies you or someone else :</u>

❖   Announce your Plan to your family that anyone that lies over the next week must fill out a Post-It Note and stick it to the refrigerator ... even the smallest one

❖   Make it fun, but keep it 'honest' ... teaching the value of honesty

❖   Let everyone know it isn't just the family members; that if you catch anyone lying outside you can fill out a Post-It note also

❖   At the end of the week, make it a 'teaching moment' by having a family meeting to discuss feelings that were experienced during this past week as a result of dishonesty.

Pants on Fire: Why Do We Tell Such Obvious, Blatant Lies?

> "Oh, what a tangled web we weave… when first we practice to deceive."
> – Walter Scott

Never has this quote been so true as today. It seems that we are barraged by personalities caught in their own webs of deception. Steve Rannazzisi recently admitted that he concocted the entire story about his experience on 9/11. Josh Duggar and many others were exposed through the Ashley Madison hack. Brian Williams was forced to admit that he lied about his experiences in Iraq.

And the deception transcends all barriers: politics, Hollywood, ministry. No segment of our culture is exempt. Why the epidemic? Why the obvious, blatant lies? Why can't we just tell the truth?

As I look at Scripture, I see that lying is as old as life itself. Whether it's Eve twisting the truth or Adam shifting responsibility or Rachel lying to her father or Jacob deceiving his brother, we see that something deep within us is simply deceptive. *"The human heart is the most deceitful of all things, and desperately wicked. Who really knows how bad it is?" (Jeremiah 17:9).*

While there is probably an infinite number of reasons why people lie, I can see three basic causes:

1 - Fear

Many people find themselves caught in a lie because of fear. Fear of the unknown. Fear of the future. Fear of what others might think. Fear of failure. Fear of who they believe they are.

I have personally allowed fear to lead me into deceit. When I suddenly found myself a single mom, I was terrified. I wondered what my future would be, who would ever love a middle-aged woman with three young children. I was afraid that my life was over, that I had lost every chance at a meaningful life. And that's when I became trapped in a deceitful lifestyle. I was controlled by fear rather than faith.

Those of us who find ourselves living in fear are in good company, however. Abraham, despite being a giant of the faith, was often caught in fear. When he left his home to go to the land God would show him, he found himself living in Egypt as a foreigner. Out of fear, he told his wife Sarai to lie to the Egyptians. Why?

> *Abram said to his wife, Sarai, "Look, you are a very beautiful woman. When the Egyptians see you, they will say, 'This is his wife. Let's kill him; then we can have her!' So please tell them you are my sister. Then they will spare my life and treat me well because of their interest in you.* Genesis 12:10-13

Despite his great faith, Abraham lied because of his fear. He lied to spare his life. He lied to gain benefits from others. And, he didn't just lie once. He didn't learn his lesson the first time. Years later, Abraham told the exact same lie to King Abimelech.

2 - Discontent

One of the last sermons my husband preached before he was caught in his adulterous relationship was on temptation. "Satan tempts us when he gets us to doubt the good gifts God has placed in our lives," he said.

How true it is. If we spend our time focusing on the things we think we should have, we begin to think that God is holding out on us, that we are missing something important. We get caught up in thinking that we should be further in our careers, have more money, own a bigger house. We miss the beautiful blessings that surround us. We fail to see that God has carefully provided for our every need and to trust that he will always be faithful.

King David was caught in the trap of discontentment. He was the king of Israel. He was wealthy, powerful. He had wives and servants. He had everything he could possibly want.

...Until he saw Bathsheba. She was beautiful, and he had to have her. Suddenly, all of God's blessings paled in comparison to this one, one who belonged to another man. But in the moment it didn't matter that she was another man's wife. He sent for her. He slept with her. His discontent caused him to seek out a forbidden relationship.

3 - Trapped by Our Own Words

Rarely do the big lies *start* as big lies. Instead, they begin as small lies. Then, more lies are heaped on top to cover those lies. Before long, we become entangled in a web of deceit, with the lies growing bigger and bigger. Before long, we can't find our way out of the mess we have created. Many times, we tell the lies so often that we begin to believe they are truth.

After David slept with Bathsheba, things went from bad to worse. Bathsheba discovered she was pregnant, and now David was left trying to cover up his sin. So he lied. He called Bathsheba's husband home from battle, encouraged him to go home to his wife. But Uriah displayed incredible integrity, refusing to engage in relations with his wife while his comrades were on the battlefield.

> *So the next morning David wrote a letter to Joab and gave it to Uriah to deliver. The letter instructed Joab, "Station Uriah on the front lines where the battle is fiercest. Then pull back so that he will be killed."* 2 Samuel 11:14-15

Lies on top of lies. A web of deceit. From adultery to murder. David was in deep, way over his head. He was trapped by his own words, his own lies.

So how do we protect ourselves from going down the path of deceit? How do we avoid becoming yet another statistic? How do we protect ourselves from the label of liar?

1 - Recognize That You are Vulnerable

When we become convinced that we are above certain sins, we put ourselves in danger. We let our guard down, becoming vulnerable. We must be constantly aware of the temptations all around us and guard our hearts and minds.

If you think you are standing strong, be careful not to fall. 1 Corinthians 10:12

2 - Become Intimate with the Truth

The best way to combat lies is to know the truth. Jesus said, "I am the Way, the Truth, and the Life" (John 14:6). Know Jesus. Spend time with God, in his Word. Saturate your mind with the truths of Scripture. Allow the word of God to penetrate your heart and mind. Be transformed by the Word of God. Believe what God has to say about you instead of the negative messages the world sends you. Defeat the father of lies (John 8:44) with the sword of the spirit.

*Don't copy the behavior and customs of this world, but **let God transform you into a new person by changing the way you think**. Then you will learn to know God's will for you, which is good and pleasing and perfect.* Romans 12:2

3 - Focus on the Eternal

Too often, we put immediate gratification over eternal rewards. We must recognize that everything on this earth is fleeting, passing away. But living God's way stores up eternal rewards.

All athletes are disciplined in their training. They do it to win a prize that will fade away, but we do it for an eternal prize. So I run with purpose in every step.... I discipline my body like an athlete, training it to do what it should. 1 Corinthians 9:25-27

Have you already been caught in a web of deception? Be thankful that our Lord is a God of redemption, and that the truth will set you free. David might have been caught in the biggest web of deceit recorded in scripture. And yet, he was known as a man after God's own heart. What separated him from other liars? What allowed him to regain a relationship with the Father?

David truly repented of his sins.

Have mercy on me, O God, because of your unfailing love. Because of your great compassion, blot out the stain of my sins. Wash me clean from my guilt. Purify me from my sin. For I recognize my rebellion; it haunts me day and night. Psalm 51:1-3

David showed through word and deed that he accepted responsibility for his actions; he changed his path. He did not despise the true friend who uncovered his lies. And God forgave, restored. And just as God forgave and restored David, he will forgive and restore you. You are never too far away from the love of God.

Dena Johnson is a busy single mom of three kids who loves God passionately. She delights in taking the everyday events of life, finding God in them, and impressing them on her children as they sit at home or walk along the way (Deuteronomy 6:7) [Source: Dena Johnson/ Publication date: September 24, 2015; http://www.crosswalk.com/print/11741834/ www.denajohnson.com]

5   Miser or Wiser?

"The Touch"

It was battered and scarred, and the auctioneer thought it scarcely worth his while to waste much time on the old violin. But he held it up with a smile:

"What am I biddin' good folks," He cried. "Who'll start the biddin' for me ? A dollar;" then, "two ! Only two ? Two dollars, and who'll make it three ? Three dollars once, three dollars twice; going for three --- " But no.

From the room, far back, a gray-haired man came forward and picked up the bow. Then, wiping the dust from the old violin, and tightening the loose strings, he played a melody pure and sweet as a caroling angel's wings.

There's many a man with life out of tune, who's battered and scarred, and is auctioned cheap to the thoughtless crowd, much like the old violin. A mess of potage, a glass of wine, a game, and he travels on. He is going once, and going twice, he's going and almost gone. But the Master comes, and the foolish crowd never can quite understand the worth of a soul, and the change that's wrought by the touch of the Master's Hand. - anonymous

"As base a thing as money often is, yet it can be transmuted into everlasting treasure. It can be converted into food for the hungry and clothing for the poor. It can keep a missionary actively winning lost men to the light of the gospel and thus transmute itself into heavenly values. Any temporal possession can be turned into everlasting wealth. Whatever is given to Christ is immediately touched with immortality."
— *A.W. Tozer (1897-1963), American pastor and writer*

How much did Our Lord, Jesus Christ have to pay the auctioneer for each and every battered and lost soul? Have you ever really considered the price that is placed on your soul both from the perspective of His plan or yours if you elect to follow your own vices? Your own game plan? Your own tune?

After Jesus was baptized by John the Baptist, He was led by the Holy Spirit to enter into a 40 day period of fasting deep into the Judean desert. [Matthew 4: 1-11] He would experience every temptation and mocking that Satan could deliver. And yet, because Jesus knew His Father's will, His voice, His commandments, He didn't flinch. Even when the Devil promised Him all the kingdoms from a mountain top, Jesus held true to His Father's words and refused his offer....'To worship His God and Serve Him only.' There was no bidding to be done on Our Savior's integrity or His purpose. Satan could not touch Him.

There is only one auctioneer for people, the devil, who starts the bidding on a soul for the superficial worldly value of a human life. A human life whose soul will be eternally lost. A human soul that will suffer intolerably for all eternity. A human life that will never know the love of His Creator. The good news for believers, is that we have the highest Bidder who sits patiently in the crowd of bidders and outbids them all for one priceless, unique soul. A soul He paid for with every droplet of blood that fell on Calvary, with every stinging scourging he tolerated, with every piercing stake driven through his wrists and ankles and every shallowed breathe before He gave up His Spirit to His Father. This is the Bidder who loved you so much that He gave up His life as an exchange Because just like the gray-haired man with that old violin, the Lord will pick each of us up, shake off the dust, tighten us up where we have fallen loose to this world and retune us to play a sweet melody as a caroling angel's wings. This tender, sweet, 'all out' generous love should be the model we all strive towards.

Yet, there is in each of us a natural tendency to be selfish from a very early age. As we learn through our parents' reaction to behavior, we are taught that crying gets us more milk, a dry diaper, a snuggle or a 3 a.m. lullaby. As we grow and mature, we learn to express ourselves in language and have much more control over negotiating outcomes. For instance, the *'toddler property law'* goes like this; (1.) If I like it, it's mine. (2). If it's in my hand, it's mine. (3). If I can take it from you, it's mine.(4). If I had it a little while ago, it's mine. (5). If it's mine, it must never appear to be yours in any way.(6). If I'm doing or building something, all the pieces are mine. (7). If it looks just like mine, it is mine. (8). If I saw it first, it's mine. (9). If you are playing with something and you put it down, it automatically becomes mine. (10) If it's broken, it's yours! Of course, as we get older, these skills are reinforced by role models and experiences and therefore, we become more selfish or we become more Christ-like.

Upon reviewing the popular *'toddler property law'*, the rules seem similar with how adults treat the ownership of 'money'; we seem to be in this "tug and pull competition" with the Lord's blessings. Remember, that everything belongs to the Lord as 2 Chronicles 29:11-12 instructs us. He is the *One* that gives us special talents to obtain a special occupation, that extends a monthly salary, that allows us to purchase assets, live in selected neighborhoods, permits our children to attend choice schools and even it is at *HIS discretion* to be promoted or not. Nothing we have comes from our own might except for what HE has deemed and favored. Yes, we have a part to be obedient, to work heartily and to possess a trustworthy character, but HE still has the final say in what happens in our circumstances. *Job* was a righteous holy man when he lost everything, including his precious family; it was not a result of sin that brought him grief. It was the Lord's discretion to do what he chose to do. The Lord can and will make decisions that will cause fear, uncertainty and anguish if we don't learn to trust His ways and become freer with our hearts' treasures, especially money. [**Matthew 6:21**]

There are over 2350 verses in the Bible that pertain to the subject of money; the subject is only second to that of "love" in the Bible. In our society, there is a competing relationship between money and love. Money, a powerful tool is often used to get what we want, rather than a supernatural act of love to give what others don't have. As believers, we are called to be 'givers', not just in our talents and time, but also in our generosity with material assets. [money, valuables, property] Even during the Holy Crusades, when mercenaries were baptized before going into battle, they were allowed to hold their swords out of the water to signify that was the one thing they could control ... *that* God had no dominion over this weapon of power. Money signifies control in our society; oftentimes, bank accounts, 401K retirement funds, and savings are marked 'exempt' from the Lord's dominion and we forget the sacred vows we promised when we were washed anew. It all belongs to HIM so we shouldn't be holding anything or anyone too tightly. And as **2 Corinthians 8:7** exhorts us to do: "Just as you excel in everything, in faith, in speech, in knowledge, in complete earnestness and in your love for us, see that you also excel in the *grace of giving*.

Let's explore scripture to clearly understand the difference between a '*miserly*' worldly attitude to that of '*giving*' or a generous attitude and the consequences both naturally and spiritually. We will start with the Parable to the Good Samaritan outlined in **Luke 10: 30-37**. A man was traveling from Jerusalem to Jericho when he was suddenly overtaken by a group of thugs who beat him senseless, stripped him of his clothing and left him near death at the side of the road. Herein lies the first worldly attitude of pure unadulterated '**greed**' & '**entitlement**' because these robbers felt that had a claim to this man's assets and integrity. <u>Rule 1: "What's Yours is Mine and I'm Going to Take it."</u>

Next, a priest traveling down the same road sees the victim but instead of coming to his assistance and offering clothing or medical attention he crosses the road to avoid him. Herein lays the second worldly attitude of if it isn't my mess or problem, , or if it's inconvenient or cost me something to help someone, then I am not getting involved. This attitude is "selfishness, miserliness, and narcissism" which runs rampant in America, the land of plenty. <u>Rule 2: "What's Mine is Mine."</u>

Yet still, another man, a Levite walks down this same road and witnesses this battered man lying in anguish, but quickly diverts to avoid the man also. Reemphasized here is the statistical fact that the majority would not get involved or get their hands dirty helping someone.

Fortunately, when the next man , a good Samaritan witnessed the man's suffering, he took pity upon him... tended to his wounds, placed him on his own donkey and took him to the nearest inn for healing. When he left the next day, he paid the inn keeper funds necessary to take care of this man and promised to reimburse him for any extra expenses incurred as a result of nurturing him. This is the "**Godly**" or "**blessed**" attitude that Jesus lived boldly when He walked the earth and *Whom* still loves generously in spite of 'selfish' tendencies from His children. It **cost** the Good Samaritan *time* [his traveling schedule was impacted by the delay of tending to this victim], *his* **comfort** in traveling [he placed the victim on his donkey and therefore, walked while allowing the man to ride], his **compassion** to stop and tend to his wounds, [he took pity and treated him with dignity] and finally his **money** [to pay the inn keeper and whatever revenue he lost due to his delayed trip as this road was heavily utilized for trade]. <u>Rule 3: "What's Mine is Yours and I'm going to Give It."</u> *{Source: Pastor Deryck Frye, Connect Community Church,, Ashland, MA. Message on Giving - "Overcoming Cardi-Cash Arrest"}*

Accordingly, these three rules listed are paralleled attitudes of giving to the house of the Lord, when it comes to tithing,[financially supporting the local church] giving to missions[to financially support the global "great commission], first fruits ,[financial blessing to spiritual leaders], alms [giving to the needy] and any special monetary need to support His Kingdom's vision.[Building projects, expansions, etc] Christians don't like to talk about tithing or giving [other than in serving]; they would rather negotiate the terms [percentage] or decline based on New Testament grace or more commonly state they simply can't afford it. *Yet,* this is not a *money issue*; it's a 'heart issue'. It isn't a *budget issue,* it's an 'attitude' issue. It isn't a *legal scripture issue* , it's a "act of 'disloyalty. Because when all is said and done, it is about how betrothed you are to Your Savior & Lord, Jesus Christ. There is no amount of money that can repay Him for the free gift of salvation. **None.** **Tithing** and **giving** joyfully towards heavenly investments are *not* checkbook entries, they are intimate 'love notes' to your Savior. The One who outbid the highest bidder, wrote a check 'paid in full' and claimed you as *His beloved.*

"Blessed"

"He is no fool who gives up what he cannot keep to gain that which he cannot lose."
— **Jim Elliot**

Therefore, we as *His beloved* should be viewing giving from the relationship perspective instead of a legal law under God. God doesn't need your money. He needs your priority in making *His* agenda first, *His* relationship first, *His* interests first, *His* Will first, *His* schedule first and *His* children first [lost or saved]. Your money is simply another extension of worship. Especially, because it is one 'power tool' that the devil uses to divert our attention to the idols of this temporary life instead of focusing on the big picture of eternity. There are two contrasting purposes for money. Choose wisely, not miserly.

Study Scriptures: {Attitudes Around Giving}

(1) **Malachi 3:10** -Bring the entire tithe into the _store house_. ... TEST ME says the Lord and See if I will not open the floodgates of _heaven_ . *This is the* **basement** *, where* **to begin** *with giving to the Lord.*

(2) **1 Cor. 13:3**   If I give all my possessions to the poor, ….but have not _Love_ ., I gain nothing. .
Acts 20:35: In everything I did, I showed you that by this kind of hard work we must help the weak, remembering the words the Lord Jesus himself said; " It is more _Bless_ to _give_ than to RECEIVE. *This is the sacrificial act of giving you do "out of love" for one another and for Your Personal Savior.*

(3) **Gal. 6:6** Anyone who receives instruction in the word must share all good things with his _teacher_ *This is a practice that is done rarely; write an encouraging note to your Pastor[s], spiritual leaders and teachers to* **let them know** *you appreciate them for their sacrifices and gifts. Be generous in gifts Appreciation goes a long way to sustain those in full time ministry.*

(4) **1 Timothy 5:17-18:** The Elders who direct the affairs of the church well are worthy of double honor, especially those whose work is teaching and preaching. …..and the worker deserves his _Wages_ These are some of the expenses at your local church that gets paid through faithful tithing of the membership, alongside Pastors, administrative staff, and other skilled workers who maintain the local church..

(5) _Gal 2:9-10:_ : Remember the _poor_. **Prov. 19:17:** One who is gracious to a poor man _lends_ to the LORD, And He will _repay_ him for his good deed. This is the giving of alms done anonymously so it doesn't cause embarrassment to the receiver. *Churches normally have general 'benevolence' accounts to give such donations.*

(6) **Mark 12:41-44:** And He sat down opposite the treasury, and *began* observing how the people were putting money into the treasury; and many rich people were putting in large sums. 42A poor

widow came and put in two small copper coins, which amount to a cent. **43**Calling His disciples to Him, He said to them, "Truly I say to you, this poor widow put in more than all the contributors to the treasury; **44**for they all put in out of their _Surplus_ , but she, out of her poverty, put in all she _owned_ , all she had to live on." *This is an example of supernatural, sacrificial giving that only happens when we possess a steadfast faith.*

(7) <u>Jer. 9:23-24:</u> The Lord says, "let not the .... _rich man_ . Boast of his riches, but let him who boasts about this: that he understands and _knows_ Me. It is at the Lord's discretion to increase wealth, but for His Will and to grow closer to that child by means of dependency. *Money should never interrupt that love..*

(8) <u>Mark 8:36:</u> : what good it is for a man to gain the whole world, yet forfeit his _Soul_ ? *Remember money is a powerful tool the devil loves to use for his gain.*

(9) <u>Matthew 6:21:</u> For where your _treasure_ is so is your _heart_ .

(10) <u>2 Cor. 9:6:</u> Whoever sows sparingly will also _reap_ sparingly, and whoever _rea. sows_ generously will also reap generously

(11) <u>Prov. 11:24-25:</u> There is one who scatters, and *yet* _increase_ all the more, And there is one who withholds what is justly due, *and yet it results* only in _want_ . The generous man will be prosperous, And he who waters will himself be water.

(12) <u>Phil 1:6:</u> _You are generous because of your faith. And I am praying that you will really put your _generosity_ to work, for in so doing you will come to an understanding of all the good things we can do for CHRIST.

A WEALTHY CHRISTIAN MAN WHO LOST EVERYTHING IN A FINANCIAL TURNDOWN WAS ASKED IF HE EVER REGRETTED ALL THE GIVING HE HAD DONE TO THE LORD'S WORK.
HE REPLIED,
"WHAT I GAVE, I STILL HAVE. WHAT I KEPT, I LOST"
anonymous

One of the most challenging changed behavior is 'tithing' and supporting 'kingdom vision' with monetary investments. Remember , your time in "ETERNITY" will be much longer than this temporary life of 70 or 80 years long. Listed below are some practical methods to start tithing to your home church.

➤   .Use a 'rounding' up method in your checkbook or Smart Phone App, so every time you deduct something...you round up to the closet whole dollar amount. _Example:_ Paid for Starbuck's Coffee that cost $.2.35 ... you would round up to $3.00 dollars instead, so 65 Cents is deducted also but that goes into a special tithing category. This will add up quickly.

➤   When you set up your auto deposit with your employer for your paycheck, automatically establish an auto-withdrawal into a separate account. You will not miss 10 %.

➤   If you cannot start at 10% due to living paycheck to paycheck, then start at a percentage you are able. However, when you get the next increase, set up the auto deduction, and honor the Lord with your blessing.

➤   Just bite the bullet and DO it. Upon receiving any income, calculate 10% and either give your 'love' offering electronically or with a check or cash.

➤   Create a "giving" journal recording your "kingdom vision" investments including tithing, first fruits, alms and planting seed. Just like you might meet with a financial adviser on how to increase your wealth, seek the Lord's heart in meeting His. You should have "giving" goals!

➤   This sounds strange, but let your home church track your giving history, so you can assess where you are at the end of the year. The important reason for this is not about filing a tax deduction, as much as it is about having goals for giving.

The word **'tithe'** means one tenth. The tithe's purpose is to be a personal testimony of the Lord's ownership in our lives. Bet you didn't know that the Old Testament Jews actually gave approximately 23% as an average for their collective tithes throughout the year for the local church, special offerings for widows and orphans and special funds for building temples, or when a need arose. [Source: "Word on Finances", Larry Burkett, 1994, p. 238]

Surely, believers today can out give them? Wait a minute. Read all about it on the next page

Below is a table of the four main types of giving that modern day believers should understand, and attempt to make as part of their 'heavenly' investment plan. The percentages are estimates based on what our Old Testament brethren normally gave. Try to make a personal chart with these four categories and plan out goals to increase in each area annually. Again, this isn't about money; it is all about your relationship with the Maker of the Universe, your personal Lord & Savior. Don't make this an obligatory rule; make it an investment into your HRA [Heavenly Retirement Account] for the "lover of your soul."

Tithe	Alms	Plant Seed	First Fruits
Equal to or more than 10%	Any Amount [5%]	Any Amount [3%]	Any Amount [5%]
Storehouse/ Local Church	Anonymously to the needy	Start Churches, mission field, gift seeding, training	Spiritual Teachers, Pastors, Disciples, Prophets, etc.
Practical Need: Pastor's & Staff Salaries, Building & Maintenance Expenses, Events, Technology, Ministries, Mission Fields	Examples: • Food Banks • Red Cross • United Way • Church Member in need	Examples: • Overseas/local new church plantings • Mission Sponsorship • Individual Gift Seed for Education/Encouragement • Training Needs •Heave or Wave Offerings	Acknowledge Blessing: • Good employees receive bonuses ..same principle • Encouragement to those that help us mature by teaching the word of God • Commitment of servitude - blessings
Ex 22:29; Gen 28:20-22; Mal 3:8-12; Mat 23:23; Luke 11:42; Heb 7:5-25; Num 18:25-28; Neh 13:5, 13	Acts 10:2; Acts 24 Mat 6:1-6; Prov 19:17; Gen 8:2; 2 Cor 9:6-11	Ezra 2:69; Prov 11:24-25; Mark 12:41; John 12:3-7; Rom 12:6, 8; Gen 33:10-11; Gen 47:11; Heb 13:16; Luke 6:31, 38; Exo 25:2-3; Amos 4:5; 3 John 8	Eze 44:30; Deut 18:4; Rom 11:16; Prov 3:9-10; Exo 22:29-30; James 1:18; Rev 14:4; Gal 6:6; 3 John 8

Yet, according to recent Pew Study[1], approximately 247 million people in the US claim to be Christian. How many of that number go to church? That's a different and more difficult number to uncover. At best, the pollsters say 40% of all Americans, or about 98 million go to church. At worst, other studies suggest 20%, or less than 50 million, actually attend and many as few as 12 times a year. However, when we analyze the attendance number, we know that, of those who do attend church, far fewer actually tithe any money.

[1source:http://christianity.about.com/od/denominations/p/christiantoday.htm]

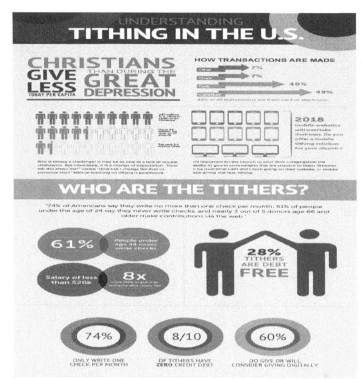

It's alarming that Christians now give less per capita than during the Great Depression. When we finally look at those in church, at best 25% of the congregation give. That's at best. If you have that level of participation, you're not in the norm, according to other research[2], which says only about 3-5% actually tithe in most cases. And, it's not the wealthy who always tithe. The statistics suggest[3] that if you make less than $20k, you're eight times more likely to give than someone who makes more than $75k.

[2Source: http://church-development.com/Quick-Stats-The%2095-Who-Dont-Tithe]

[3source: http://healthresearchfunding.org/21-tithing-statistics/] [Source: http://www.sharefaith.com/blog/2015/12/facts-christians-tithing/]

Goals to Set - *The Attitude of your Giving — Luke 12:34*

If you haven't started tithing , write down the reasons why you haven't been able to start?

(1) What will you have to do to start tithing fully @ 10% ?

   i. What other sacrificial giving have you done in your Christian walk similar to the widow and the miter?

   ii. What is the hardest thing to give up? What is the easiest thing to give up? Why?

Use your Journal to record these thoughts

❖ Write a Post-It note for every purposeful giving you start this week
❖ Write a Post-IT note with an encouraging note to a co-worker
❖ Write a Post-It note for anyone who gave something to you this week [doesn't have to be monetary]
❖ Write an encouraging note / card to your Pastor, Pastor's family member, spiritual teacher/leader, prophet or just someone who has made an impact in your life spiritually

The Father Who Gave His Most Precious Possession

There once was a father who loved his children, but they didn't love him. One after another left their father's house, vowing never to return. Finally, the father had a son who reciprocated that love. This son honored, respected, and obeyed his father. The father was thrilled, but he still mourned over his other children who had rejected him. He then came up with a plan – a risky plan: "I will give up my beloved son to make room in my house for my wayward children to return. Hopefully, they will realize my love for them and come back home."

You may recognize this vignette as the story told in the book of John:

*For God so loved the world that he gave his one and only Son, that whoever believes in him shall not perish but have eternal life. – **John 3:16 NIV***

No list of extraordinary giving stories could be complete without including this one. I hope you agree.

[source: https://christianpf.com/extraordinary-stories-about-giving]/

The Theocratic Economic "Model" to that of a Capitalist World Economy.

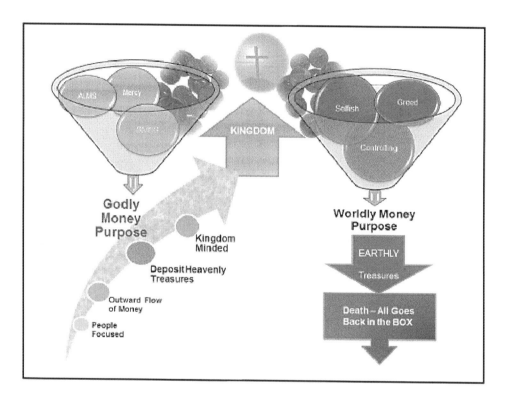

6   Paycheck or Calling?

What's your Bailywick ? ....
It is estimated that only 25-30% of Americans are
happy, fully engaged, satisfied and find purpose in
their current occupation. According to a recent study
published by the Dale Carnegie Training Center, the number
one reason for satisfaction in a job is that the employee *feels*

valued, has *opportunity for growth* and *advancement* to be part of something *greater than themselves*. It
claimed three key drivers: (1) Relationship with immediate supervisor (2) Belief in senior leadership and
(3) Pride in working for the company.*[source: http://www.huffingtonpost.com/2013/07/11/why-people-hate-jobs_n_3579873.html]*

Still yet, another international study done by the **The Happiness Research Institute**, in Copenhagen,
conducts an ongoing study that drills into the sources of personal and professional contentment. Once
the basics of safety, civility, and fair wages are met, what matters most? Number One is a *sense of
purpose*. *Purpose* contributes twice as much to an individual's job satisfaction as the runner-up, which is
having a *high-quality manager.[Source: http://www.huffingtonpost.com/sarah-finnie-robinson/happy-work-happy-life_b_9573780.html]*

Hmmmm, interesting. What is missing from many people's assumption that it's *just about the
money*? The pursuit of more money, although it appeared in the following 'top 10' reasons is *not* at the
Top:

10. They think the grass is greener someplace else. If your employee's friends are having an amazing
experience at another company, why wouldn't they be envious? The transparency of employee benefits
and perks at other companies can sometimes lead your employees to dream about working elsewhere.
Keep an eye on what other companies are doing and try to match where you can. Sure, your company's
perks aren't going to be on par with Google, but why not try to give your employees something worth
bragging about? They'll be more motivated, eager to spread the good word, and you'll benefit from an
improved company culture.

9. Their values don't align with the company. Dissatisfaction is bound to take place if your employees
aren't sold on the same things you are. If your company values creativity and collaboration, it's in your
best interest to make screening for these values a mandatory part of your hiring process. Regular
feedback and reviews can help you stay in tune with employees' values and how they align with what
the company needs and values most.

8. They don't feel valued. If you aren't taking the time to pat your employees on the back, it's bound to
impact employee happiness. Recognition breeds feelings of value and loyalty. What are you doing to
show your employees they're valued members of the company? This doesn't mean giving monetary
rewards for every accomplishment—instead, regularly utilize verbal praise and offer the occasional gift
or reward for awesome performance.

7. **Job insecurity.** It's easy to dislike your job when you're worried whether you will still have it a few months or a year from now. If your company is going through hard times, the instability may be taking a toll on your employees. Remain transparent and work on keeping spirits high and your team engaged...or they might end up leaving you out of fear.

6. **There's no room for advancement.** What's your company's policy for promotions? Many employees end up feeling stuck when there's no chance of advancing within their company. This often leads to job hopping. Your company may be small, but it's important to create a plan for employees to grow with you.

5. **They're unhappy with their pay.** Nothing extinguishes passion quite like the feeling of being paid less than you deserve. Evaluating the salaries of your employees can be unrealistic at certain times, but you should consider asking your employee what they feel they should be making — their honesty may surprise you.

4. **There's too much red tape.** Rules may be ruining your team. Nothing is more frustrating than being unable to make your own decisions. Boost the autonomy of your employees by giving them room to accomplish goals. This establishes a healthy level of trust, productivity, and benefits the company as a whole.

3. **They're not being challenged.** Your employees are on a constant search to advance their skills and improve through their work with you. A lack of meaningful, challenging work is certain to breed disdain. Find out whether your employees feel like they're learning or advancing their knowledge. If they're not becoming better, they will go someplace where they feel they can improve.

2. **The passion's gone.** There's a huge difference between living to work and working to live. Do your employees love what they do? The current job climate has led many people to take on jobs they don't love. Focus on hiring thoroughly passionate employees and giving them a purpose to maintain their passion throughout their time on the job.

1. **Their boss has poor leadership skills:.** Poor management can ruin even the most passionate and well-paid employees love for their job. Don't let your awful management and leadership skills ruin the drive of your workforce. Do you micromanage and criticize? Are you a bad communicator? If you have unhappy employees, the first thing you should look at is your management habits. The next thing to do is actually talk to your employees to get to the bottom of the problem.
[http://www.huffingtonpost.com/2013/07/11/why-people-hate-jobs_n_3579873.html]

So, how can you remain a faithful steward and light in the workplace if you feel unvalued, berated and unchallenged? Let's take a honest look through the guiding filter of scripture to navigate through the challenges of dissatisfaction in your job. . Fortunately, God's word has answers for every problem listed above. As you read the solutions in the following, please read the scriptures referenced. Questions will follow.

(1) <u>Your Boss is a Poor Leader:</u> unfair, moody, insecure, lies to promote themselves, throws others under the bus because they never take the accountability. <u>Your Part:</u> Submit to the authority that is over your life. That includes bad bosses. <u>2 Peter 2:18-23</u>-When treated unfairly by a superior, we should submissively endure by entrusting ourselves to God, the righteous Judge. <u>God's Part:</u>

HE is the Judge over all matters and He will vindicate the situation. Maybe, not in the timing you would like, but eventually justice will be served if you take your hand off HIS gavel. **Colossians 3:23-24** You serve the Lord and not man, so think of it in these terms; you don't report to your bad boss ... you actually report to the LORD. When you clock in or enter that workplace, you are working heartily for the Lord. Read about Joseph's Godly handling of his unfair treatment by those that had authority over him including family in Genesis 37-39 and how he reacted in grace, mercy and an purposeful act of forgiveness we should all yearn to possess as believers. On the other side of this coin, is the believer's role as a "leader" Whether or not, you are a leader in title or position, you can lead from wherever you serve. [work] **Romans 14:12**. Be Accountable in even the smallest tasks.

(2) **Passion's Gone:** *Calling or Vocation?* **Your Part:** *What would you do if you were not paid any money?* Hopefully, you took one of the vocation assessment tests in Chapter 1. That should give you a good idea on what your natural aptitudes are. Passion and purpose are kinsmen, so if you figure out what you really love to do and then stick to it, there will be ultimate success. Ask other believers , friends, family what they think you would be proficient at doing. Seek a vocation counselor to help determine your placement in the marketplace, but above all seek the Lord's guidance in your purpose for this life.[**Prov. 20:5, Prov. 19:21, 1 Pet 2:15**] **God's Part:** The Lord gave us all a set of unique abilities to enable us to work to provide for our loved ones, but He is also a passionate God that wants us to find true contentment .[**Jer 29:11**]- *"Employ whatever God has entrusted you with, in doing good, all possible good, in every possible]kind and degree." John Wesley*

(3) **Not Challenged at Work:** Tedious, routine, boring, yawn-ville work. **Your Part:** Step Up and suggest or ask for more challenging work [you should be able to describe the next step], so your manager knows you are interested in more difficult work. This shows initiative and that is rare in our work environments today. Volunteer to work on a new project, go back to school and gain a different skill, certification or talent that you might be missing from your team that is needed. The worse scenario could be you get turned down, but you just introduced a Godly attitude by offering to help beyond your job description. Go the extra mile. If you do, you will be in the minority. And if this doesn't work, then seek more challenging work; you may have reached your ceiling in this job. [**2 Cor. 8:17**] *Titus went on his own volition to Corinth; he was eager to serve so noone had to convince him.* **God's Part:** He is a gracious God that wants you to be productive, mature and rise to your God-given potential. He longs to be gracious to you. [**Isa. 30:18**]

(4) **Too much Red Tape/Rules :** typical environment of a controlling, micro-managing culture. **Your Part:** obey them as you are under the authority of the company's procedures and policies. Volunteer to be on an employee committee or suggest an employee suggestion box for continual improvement ideas. Be a leader and change what you can with respect. [**Eph. 4:23**] **God's Part:** To rework your attitude about little annoyances like these in the workplace. Rules are abundant everywhere. It shows a sign of disrespect by bucking rules. Therefore, God's word is provided to renew your *stinking thinking* to get your attitude straight.. {**Rom. 12:2**]

(5) **Unhappy with your Pay:** Depending on your current situation this could be something you can change by your performance, your finding new employment or increasing your skill set. Sometimes, it is the company's salary limitations, [cash flow], or the job market that pays higher

for those jobs harder to fill. Whatever the situation is, you have a choice With higher wages, comes more responsibility and oftentimes, more hours of dedication to meet the new accountability. Be aware of wielding ambition that could ultimately lead to unbalance in other areas of your life, especially relationships with the Lord and family. [Rom. 2:6-8]. **God's Part:** It is at the Lord's discretion to promote, create wealth or make poor, to humble or to promote. [1 Sam. 2:7]

(6) **No Room for Advancement:** Same as Non Challenging work or Pay Dissatisfaction._IN Practical terms, you can choose to seek another job where there are opportunities, or make yourself promotable by seeking other challenging work. Get out of your comfort zone. Like the sick man beside the Bethesda pool, you have to want to do something to change your situation Never underestimate seasons of waiting because God is always preparing you for the next.

(7) **Job Insecurity:** Rumor of company layoffs are common place these days. **Your Part**: There are few loyal employers that take care of their dedicated employees any longer, so it is important that you learn the basics in this Bible class and follow the principles of saving for unforeseen emergencies, having fluid assets [items you can sell] and long term investment reserves. **God's Part:** He takes care of our needs always and it oftentimes during these valleys that our faith is tried and sanctified.. [Matt. 6:26, Ps. 139:10]

(8) **Feeling Unvalued:** We feel under-valued if we give power to other's opinions of us instead of looking in the mirror and seeing the Godly reflection that God desires. This is not a free card out of 'self-reflection' salon either! **Your Part:** You have to have some close friendships with Godly people to give you honest feedback of shortcomings, however, you should cautiously consider the source when feeling unworthy in the workplace. So much of this one is subjective, so that is why you need an objective friend to level set your reality. Oftentimes, this is a hostile or dysfunctional culture that is not healthy to stay. However, it could be a fertile ground for 'shining your light' and bringing the joy of the Lord front and center. You are a soldier of His now, so get ready for some challenging assignments.. [Matt. 5:16, Ps.139 :13-16] **God's Part:** He died on a Cross for you... to give you *eternal value*..[John 3:16]

(9) **Values don't Align:** This can be a show stopper for a believer as we glean our values from the word of God and walking that out. **Your Part:** Make sure to screen the companies you are potentially interested in pursuing opportunities. Obviously, there are occupations that fall outside a believer trying to walk in the truth and righteousness of God's word. [James 1:22, Eph 5:7-14]. **God's Part:** The Lord has provided clear instruction of living a sanctified, or "set apart" life, yet not isolated so we spread His good News baptizing nations. [Acts 13:47, Mat. 28:18].

(10) **Think it is better somewhere else**: In Biblical terms, this is covetous, desiring something that someone else has. Dreaming that if the 'what ifs' came true, you would have contentment. This are dangerous grounds for Christians. **Your Part**: Learn to be contented in whatever circumstance you find yourself. Otherwise, you will always seek more, more, more ... that of which is unquenchable. [Phil. 4:6-7, Ex.20:17] **God's Part:** He understands your needs, the condition of the human heart, so He is forgiving for all of your shortcomings. However He still wants a relationship with us in prayer, worship and yes, even while we work, so we need to

meditate on His word to solve the issues of this life. Because there isn't a greener pasture than the one that's prepared for us in Our Heavenly home. [Matt. 6:26]

Study Scriptures:

(1) **What is your Number 1 Work related issue that is listed in the top ten?** Explain both in practical terms and Biblical terms [List a Scripture verse] how you will address that.

(2) **Who do you really work for?.** How will this attitude change your perspective?

Lst for the Lord

(3) **Have you figured out what your calling is for the Lord in practical terms?** Explain how your calling compliments your vocation?

(4) _**So many of our challenges in life have to do with our attitude; list below with a memory verse how you will transform your mind?** *Romanos 8:28*

(5) **Read.Luke 20: 19-26:** When you work in an industry like construction or other types of "cash under the table", do you have an accountability to pay taxes on that income? Why or why not? List a couple reasons.

Let's Get Practical - THE ART OF BUSY-NESS

(1)   In our busy society we juggle so many balls that we are living very fragmented, hurried lives with a sobering emptiness that leaves us weary. We justify running the kid's to different sports, clubs, activities, lessons for the reasoning of excellent parenting. We attend

Stop the glorification of busy.

PTA meetings, get involved with community marches, sign up for fund raising, volunteer at church events and are crowding the town hall meetings. We are involved. We, of course, make time to have "date nights" with our spouses, have a movie / game night with our children and perhaps, a special visit to grandmother in the nursing home. We are living life at the rate of nanoseconds, hurrying from one stop to another forgetting to "stop and pause". To reflect. To Meditate on His word. To Pray. To Worship alone. And to watch God's glory cresting the horizon bleeding crimsons as if to say "good morning". **Time** does not stop. You **must** to hear God's voice and direction in your life. Let's do an exercise in assessing how we are doing in this area of balancing the natural busy-ness in contrast to the spiritual preparation that will take you and your family into eternity with your Maker.

➤ .For this exercise, track one week or more, in percentages, what time was spent in each category. Oh, and remember to track how much sleep, exercise, reading, downtime, electronics [smart phones, laptops, notepads, game devices, etc., watching TV … and of course how much time you spent praying, worshipping and studying the word of God [outside the four walls of your home church]. If you have other significant categories that are not included in the diagram, feel free to add them. Basically, over the course of the week it all has to add up to 100% of your time. [Smart Phone Apps to help this tracking try either Sectograph or Time Meter to see the results at the end of the week] Also, draw a line from GOD being in the center to all other activities that are directly related.

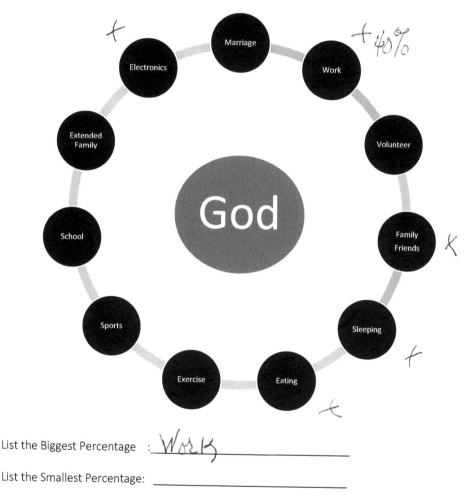

List the Biggest Percentage : _WORK_

List the Smallest Percentage: _____

What if anything will you change in your life to try and balance your daily life activities?

The Two Income Trap has only gotten worse: America has become a dual-income nation since one income isn't enough to maintain a household. America has become a nation where households depend on **multiple streams of income just to get by**. Many people think that having two incomes is a luxury when in most cases, you need two incomes just to get by and keep up with the rising cost of living. This is reflected in the two income trap. Take for example a couple that works and makes the median household income of $52,000. In many cases if the couple has a child, daycare costs are needed and these can run exceptionally high. Healthcare costs are also incredibly high and have grown unbelievably fast over the last two decades. This recent recession could have been called a <u>Mancession since most of the jobs lost went to men</u>. America is a nation of dual-income households because people are too broke to get by on one income. The current state of the economy hasn't helped much in supporting economic growth for working families.

Back in 1965 47% of families had both spouses working. That figure is now up to 66% and it is extremely rare to find a household where only the husband works. You also find it more common today that a household will have only the wife working.

Women entering the workforce has shifted how people deal with daily life. But the thought of economic freedom by having an additional income in the household has been largely swept away by **inflation**. Take a look at this chart:

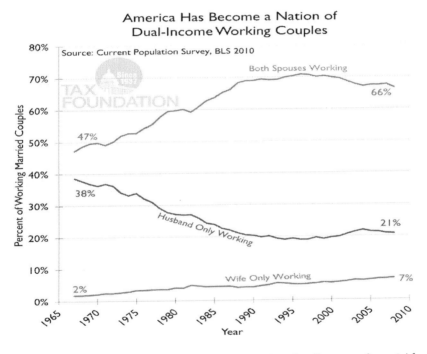

You would think that this would be providing American families more financial freedom but instead it is merely keeping people from being out on the streets. The homeownership rate is now down to generational lows. Why? Because home prices are inflated thanks to banking policies and investors that have gutted the market and have created a shortage of housing for working families. <u>So what is left is higher rents and higher home prices.</u>

We expect the homeownership rate to bottom at 63.5% in 2016

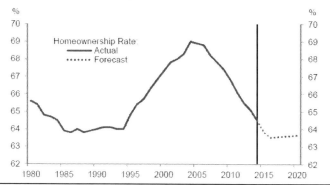

Source: Census Bureau, Goldman Sachs Global Investment Research.

In 1950 typical healthcare costs ran about $1,000 per year adjusting for inflation. Today they run over $10,000 per year and this isn't factoring a serious illness or injury. This is merely to have routine insurance coverage for your family.

More money does not mean more flexibility if inflation is eating away the cost of living. With two working people, you have more money spent on childcare, food, and it is very likely that two cars are necessary with people commuting to separate jobs. Cars eat up a lot of money in payments, gas, and maintenance. In the end, you have a large amount of unexpected expenses that eat away at that additional paycheck.

This is the trap. You have two incomes so why are people struggling more today than that single income from the 1950s and 1960s? In short the **answer is inflation** and the destruction of our manufacturing base. There is a race to the bottom in this low wage economy. The middle class is now a minority and the two income trap is even getting harder to dig out of. This is why people are so angry during this election because there really isn't a champion for the middle class.

People do have options to make things better and being able to **budget is absolutely critical**. Many couples also buy homes that are beyond their **means just to keep up with the Joneses**. And you absolutely need to plan for retirement. Don't be like many that are using the "work until you die" model of retirement. The two income trap may make things hard but don't compound your financial problems with inadequate planning. *[Source: http://www.mybudget360.com/two-income-trap-working-couples-married-couples-working-percent-income-to-keep-up/]*

If you lost one income if married or if single your only income, what is your Plan B?
(1)   What would be your first step of action?
(2)   Who would you contact, if anyone to share the news? *My sister, daughters*
(3)   What would be the biggest challenge if you lost 50% or all your income for 8
months?
Use your Journal to record these thoughts

Post It Activity

<u>Stick a post it note to everything you could sell if you needed to raise cash!:</u>
   ❖   Write a Post-It note for a business you could start with little or no overhead?
   ❖   Write a Post-It note for every LinkedIn contact you have that could be a
reference to get you a job where they work [or a list
of references]
   ❖   Write a Post-IT note citing a memory verse that
will get you through this valley if you are in a dead-end
job, under a 'nasty' boss, or in a hostile environment where the
culture is negative and depressing. If you are in a dream job, but
you would like to make more money, cite a memory verse that
will keep your focus on the end target. Hint: many to choose from
the earlier reading in this chapter.

> *"Don't get so busy making a living that you forget to make a life."*
>
> **Dolly Parton**

ROCKS, PEBBLES AND SAND

A philosophy professor stood before his class with some items in front of him. When class began, he wordlessly picked up a large empty mayonnaise jar and proceeded to fill it with rocks about two inches in diameter. He then asked the students if the jar was full. They agreed that it was.

The professor then picked up a box of pebbles, poured them into the jar and lightly shook it. The pebbles, of course, rolled into the open areas between the rocks. The students laughed. He asked his students again if the jar was full. They agreed that it was.

The professor then picked up a box of sand and poured it into the jar. Of course, the sand filled up everything else.

"Now," said the professor, "I want you to recognize that this is your life. The rocks are the important things—your family, your partner, your health, your children—anything that is so important to you that if it were lost, you would be nearly destroyed. The pebbles are the other things in life that matter, but on a smaller scale. The pebbles represent things like your job, your house, your car. The sand is everything else—the small stuff.

"If you put the sand or the pebbles into the jar first, there is no room for the rocks. The same goes for your life. If you spend all your energy and time on the small stuff, material things, you will never have room for the things that are truly most important. Pay attention to the things that are critical in your life. Play with your children. Take your partner out dancing. There will always be time to go to work, clean the house, give a dinner party and fix the disposal."

Wise words. In your own life, be sure to take care of the rocks first—the things that really matter. Remember, the rest is only pebbles and sand. *-Anonymous.*

I love this

7   Penny Wise and Pound Foolish!

"Penny Wise and Pound Foolish" is an expression started approximately in 1600 by Robert Burton, an British author. It simply means when people go to great lengths to save pennies yet they lose a greater amount due to foolish and extravagant purchases.. It kind of parallels with the old phrase "cutting off your nose in spite of your face".

> " 'If I see a madman driving a car into a group of innocent bystanders then I cannot simply, as a Christian, wait for the catastrophe then comfort the wounded and bury the dead. I must wrestle the steering wheel out of the hands of the driver.."
> - Dietrich Bonhoeffer

Some examples of this expression are listed below:
- ✓ Parking in a metered spot without paying the quarter, because you are dashing in and out to find out upon your return, there is a ticket for $10.00.
- ✓ Avoiding regular physical check-ups and then developing a serious ailment that was avoidable or easier to battle if only you had been seen earlier.
- ✓ Coupon clipping, and then traveling to five different stores to get all those savings, but not considering the gas cost was far more than the savings.
- ✓ Driving across town to save 10 cents a gallon on gasoline, but drives a BMW which they cannot afford.
- ✓ S A L E.....Saving 25% on many items, but paying with a credit card bearing an interest rate of 33% eradicating all savings unless you pay off before the interest kicks in. .
- ✓ Purchasing a home with a mortgage so beyond an affordable range that one becomes 'house poor', since the payment is so high.
- ✓ Even the United States' bureaucratic government with cutting budgets from the arts or social programs that could potentially cause greater loss for generations to come.
- ✓ Have you ever requested bids from three different contractors and selected the lowest price to only be sorely disappointed by the quality or worse, undone work?
- ✓ Paying welfare to people which is costing this country tremendous *lost potential* of purpose, gifts and contribution to the national economy as well as the self-actualization of the recipient.
- ✓ Law written to protect the liberties of *some* to remove *all* liberties from voiceless thousands. [abortion]
- ✓ Law passed that would establish standards for the majority, when it is based on the demands of the minority. [IE...Transgender bathrooms]

Being short-sighted in how we spend our money doesn't encourage saving or investing for the future needs naturally, emotionally and/or spiritually. This also applies to our perspectives on many aspects of our lives as believers. What are the little foxes that can destroy the vineyard? What are you doing now for the next twenty, thirty, or forty years? Oftentimes, during counseling sessions with people seriously in debt, it is hardly ever the popular cliché ... "well, if you just cut the Starbuck Latte's" or "even those designer bags from QVC" .from your spending plan, you will be fine." It is the mortgage that is accounting for 45% or more of their overall budget, or that 'project car being restored' costing thousands of dollars, or that gambling addiction that not only is playing with God's blessing, but creating the 'perfect storm' of emotional turmoil and breakdown of an otherwise good marriage. Or worse yet, a series of lies between spouses that leads to divorce. Remember money speaks power especially in marriage. . Big outcomes require big changes now.

If you want to be healthy in your sixties, you need to start exercising, eating a balanced diet, avoiding risky behavior, and maintaining a weight recommended by health professionals in your twenties. So, to have investments in the future, you will have to do the same thing...prepare now, develop a long term plan, stick to it and watch it grow. And "Millennials" and "Generation Z", it is 'prime time' for anyone between 18-33 years old, to start sticking to the suggested 70/30 budget outlined in chapter 2. If you establish a habit at an early age, you won't have to worry about having sufficient retirement or savings when you will need it later in life. Start NOW. As for the rest of us over the age of 33, restructure your budget so you can start tending to your investments and savings. Tap into matching funds that 401Ks with your employer yields; it is FREE money! If your employer doesn't offer a retirement plan, then start one; meet with a financial planner and start contributing to an Individual Retirement Account. Automatically have funds taken out of your paycheck directly into savings account.

Additionally, if you are receiving a 'refund' from the Internal Revenue Service over $200.00, then you need to go to www.irs.gov and use their withholding calculator to figure out how many credit exemptions you can claim to yield the smallest refund at the end of the calendar year. Otherwise, you are lending your money to the government. Plain and Simple. The government does not pay *any interest* on that 'refund' money', so why not add your cash flow to your overall budget to allow you to start savings and/or an investment? You will receive an actual return on your money. Learn to manage your money to your benefit.

12 Jaw-Dropping Statistics About Retirement
By *Matthew Frankel*

In general, Americans haven't done a great job of saving for retirement. While there are many people who have done a good job, and the early indication is that the younger generations are doing a better job than older generations did, the overall picture of retirement savings in America doesn't look too good. With that in mind, here are 12 statistics that show where we stand.

One in three Americans has nothing saved for retirement.
(1) According to a survey from GOBBankingRates.com, one out of every three Americans have absolutely nothing saved for retirement, 56% have less than $10,000 saved, and just 18% have $200,000 or more in retirement savings.

The average 50-year-old has $60,000 saved for retirement.
(2) This is a little scary. It's not that big of a problem when a 30-year-old has no significant retirement savings, as they still have time to fix the problem. However, 50-year-olds aren't so fortunate. The average 50-year-old's retirement savings of $60,000 is nowhere near enough to provide enough income to live on, even assuming it grows significantly between now and retirement.

Only 18% of workers say they're "very" confident about having enough money for a comfortable retirement; 24% are "not at all" confident.

(3) Given the statistics stated earlier, this shouldn't come as too much of a surprise. After all, if we're not saving money, how can we expect to live a comfortable life once we're no longer working and earning a paycheck?

The U.S. retirement savings gap is estimated to be between $6.8 trillion and $14 trillion.

(4) Research from the National Institute on Retirement Security found that the difference between what Americans have saved and what they *should* have saved is in the trillions of dollars. Even with the broadest definition of "savings" including things like home equity, the savings gap is at least $6.8 trillion.

Only 25% of people say they don't plan to work in retirement.

(5) According to a survey by Bankrate.com, most Americans plan to work during retirement, and just one-fourth say they have no plans to do so. To be fair, this includes people who plan to work because they like to work or because work keeps them busy and motivated. However, 62% of those who plan to work after retirement cited a financial motivation.

$30,000 in student loan debt can mean $325,000 less in retirement savings.

(6) This statistic should be on the minds of millennials as they decide on a student loan repayment plan. A recent report[1] found that millennials who have $30,000 in student loan debt at the start of their careers, on average, can expect to have $325,000 less in retirement savings, when compared to peers who start with no debt. Of course, this can still work out in your favor if your degree significantly improves your earnings potential, but it's worth considering.

[Source:www.Limra.com/posts//PR/Industry_trends_blog/LIMRA/Secure_Retirement_Institute_$30,000_in_school_loan_Debt_could_mean_$325,000_in_lost_retirement_savings.aspx]

One-fourth of employees are refusing *free money.*

(7) Americans are missing out on $24 billion every year in matching contributions from their employers. Why? Millions of people are not saving enough in their 401(k) to take full advantage of their employer's matching contribution. These employees are *losing out on $1,336 per year, on average, in free money.*

Millions more aren't aware of the Saver's Credit.

(8) The Saver's Credit, formally known as the Retirement Savings Contributions Credit, is one of the best tax benefits available to low- and moderate-income taxpayers. Here's a full description [source: , but in a nutshell, the credit can be worth up to $2,000 per couple in free money, just for saving for retirement. Only 25% of American workers who would qualify based on income are even aware of this credit.

[Source: https://www.fool.com/retirement/2016/12/03/the-savers-tax-credit-free-money-to-save-for-retir.aspx

]

The average Social Security check for a retired worker is $1,355 per month, as of Nov. 2016.

(9) This translates to an income of $16,260 per year. Sure, it's nice to have this guaranteed, inflation-protected income stream. However, could you imagine living on *just* this amount of money?

47% of single seniors and 22% of married couples are almost completely dependent on Social Security.

(10) Social Security is only meant to be one form of retirement savings. In fact, the Social Security Income says that Social Security is intended to replace 40% of the average retiree's income. However, far too many people are almost completely reliant on Social Security.

55% of retirees stopped working earlier than expected.

(11) If your retirement savings plan involves you working until 70 years old to build up a nest egg, you may want to come up with a backup plan. Mainly because of health reasons or job loss, 55% of retirees stopped working before they planned. The average retirement age is about 63 years old, so keep this in mind when crafting a savings plan.

62 for me

A retired couple can expect to spend about $260,000 during retirement on healthcare alone.

(12) The latest estimates from Fidelity found that the average 65-year-old couple retiring this year will need $260,000 to cover healthcare expenses in retirement. And this doesn't include nursing home care, if you end up needing it.

[Source: https://www.fidelity.com/viewpoints/retirement/retiree-health-costs-rise]

What you can do if your savings aren't what they should be

If you're one of the millions of Americans who haven't been doing a great job of saving for retirement, there's no better time to turn things around than right now. Take advantage of the retirement savings options available to you, such as IRAs and your employer's 401(k) and make it a priority to save as much as you can, as soon as you can. You may be surprised at the effect of a seemingly small contribution increase over the long run.

The $16,122 Social Security bonus most retirees completely overlook

If you're like most Americans, you're a few years (or more) behind on your retirement savings. But a handful of little-known "Social Security secrets" could help ensure a boost in your retirement income.

[Source: https://www.fool.com/retirement/2017/01/01/12-jaw-dropping-stats-about-retirement.aspx]

Even though, Americans are anxious about the **"golden years"** with the diminishing returns on their 401Ks from the 2008 economic upheaval and watching the value of their homes plummet due to the insane and nearly criminal mortgage notes being sold to *willing* debtors, there is still hope when you tap into what the word of God tells us. You will find it is once again about **balance**, in the natural and the spiritual facets of your life.

The **"Parable of the Rich Fool"** found in <u>Luke 12:13-34</u> illustrates what happens when 'short-sightedness' action leads to an attitude of greed, entitlement and foolishness. As the parable starts, a brother to the rich man asks Jesus to tell his rich brother to give him his inheritance. Jesus quickly rebuked the brother for making such a request and warned him against his attitude of *entitlement.* Jesus stated," *Watch out! Be on your guard against all kinds of greed; a man's life does not consist in the* *abundance of his possessions."* To restate his message again, Jesus proceeded to retell a story of a rich man that had developed a very selfish attitude about the blessings from the Lord.

A rich farmer had harvested a bumper crop and actually ran out of room to store the excess, so he decided to tear down his barns, replace them with larger barns and then just sit back and "live on the fat of the land." You see, the rich farmer had decided to sit back in his rocker, retire early from this labor and enjoy his state of 'self-contentment'. *God exhorted,* "You fool, this very night your life will be taken and then who do you think will get all of this?"

Lessons to take from this Parable: [Please read these verses]:
- ✓ **Hard work** that produces wealth [surplus] is *not* the issue here; this man had forgotten where the blessings came from. **[1 Chron. 29:10-16, Haggai 2:8, Deut. 8:18, 1 Sam 2:7]**
- ✓ **Wealth** itself is *not* the problem; it was 'what' the rich man *didn't do* with his money to further the kingdom of God and His people. **[Prov. 3:9-10, 1 Tim. 6:8, Prov. 11:24, Deut. 15:10, Acts 20:35]**
- ✓ No one in the Bible *except* for the Levite Priests **[Numbers 8:23-26]** ever **retired**; they did so at the age of 50 because the work was laborious, but then they mentored the younger men taking over their roles. There is nothing wrong with retiring from your job, but the Bible *never encourages* anyone to retire from the Lord's Work. The rich man clearly was lost in his own pleasures and comfort.
- ✓ The rich farmer was missing one huge priority in his state of 'narcissism' ... that all these riches get handed off to someone else upon his death. Whether, it is his creditors, the state or some distant relative that appears suddenly, he is not taking any of this with him to the grave. **[Job 1:21, Ecc. 5:15]**
- ✓ The saddest part of this parable is that the rich man didn't understand the gravity of dying and standing before the Judge, the Lord God. *"What does it profit a man to gain the world yet forfeit your soul?"* Having a personal relationship with Jesus Christ is the number one priority in the life as a believer; if you hold that dear and commit to growing, other relationships will fall in place with your heart of intentions and your fruits will be measured by the treasures you honor. **[Mark 8:35-37, Ecc. 9:10, Rev. 2:4]**

John Ortberg, a Christian Pastor and Author wrote a book titled, "It all goes back in the Box". He emphasizes the need for us to take a careful review of our priorities as we are trekking through this journey called "life". That there exists this **"Unscratchable Itch"** because we live in a culture of *'more'*. In Ecclesiastes, Solomon states in **Chapter 4: 10**, that "Whoever loves money never has money enough; Whoever loves wealth is never satisfied with his income. This too is meaningless." Now, Solomon had no need for money; he

> "We are all against materialism. We don't want to be materialistic! We just want more." -
>
> John Ortberg

was the wealthiest man in the Bible. Yet he held the truth of what matters at the end of one's life in **Chapter 12: 13-14,** to ..."Fear God and keep His commandments....For God will bring every deed into judgment...every hidden thing, whether good or evil." *[Source: "IT all goes back in the Box, John Ortberg, p. 190-192, 2007]*

So, there isn't anything wrong to save, invest; to acquire wealth; that would contradict what the Bible teaches, but there must be **balance** in how tightly you clench that money. Do you hoard it like the rich farmer in the parable or do you give abundantly like the spirit filled N.T. believers did in **Acts 4:31-35**? What would the Kingdom landscape look like if we collectively as 'born again' Christians gave to promote the well-being of others, sacrificed the latest model vehicle to feed a thousand children in a war torn third world country, set up savings not only for Christmas gifts, but also for the purpose of supporting a missions trip, or established an 'investment' portfolio for Heaven's return on lost souls? We are all given a different set of skills and resources; if we are given more talents, wealth, knowledge, time , then we are accountable to give more thereby glorifying God. [Luke 12:48] It is an act of reciprocity. It's like saying, "Thank-you Lord for the blessings of all these gifts so I can benefit others." If you are not consistently investing with eternity as the backdrop, you are being 'short-sighted' in the ultimate goal as a believer.

Watch **Francis Chan's Rope Illustration** on YouTube: **https://youtu.be/jF_x8dsvb_4** [It is the 5 minutes & 58 minutes long]

Study Scriptures:

(1) Prov. 21:20, Gen. 41:34-36, 1 Tim 5:8   What are some reasons for saving?

- ❖ *reserve when there isn't.*
- ❖ *provide for himself and household*
- ❖ *tesoro precioso hay en la casa del sabio pero el hombre necio lo disipa (mal gasta)*

(2) Ecc. 5:13-15, Ecc. 11:1-2, Prov. 13:11, Prov. 21:5 . . How does gambling contradict the scriptural principles of working hard and being a faithful steward of the Lord's possessions?

- ❖ *Wealth gain by dishonesty will be diminished But he who gathers by labor will increase.*
- ❖ *The plans of the diligent lead surely to plenty But those of everyone who is hasty surely to poverty.*
- ❖ *Riches kept for there owner to his ruit. He shall take nothing from his labor.*

— Give

(3) List some principles below for investing. [Matthew 25: 14-30] Why do you think each man profits accordingly to his ability of managing the money? What is the take-away here?

La parabola de los talentos :
- ❖ El que Dios le dio 5 - le devolvio los 5 + 5 mas.
- ❖ El que Dios le dio 5 - le devolvio los 2 + 2 mas
- ❖ El que le dio 1 - lo enterro

Porndlo donde gana intereses.

Here are some financial formulas that every wise manager over their money should know and understand.

"Compound interest is the eighth wonder of the world. He who understands it, earns it ...
he who doesn't ...
pays it."

— **Albert Einstein**

(2) Compound Interest:

The formula for annual compound interest, including principal sum, is:

$$A = P(1 + r/n)^{(nt)}$$

$100 \left(1+1\right)^{1} = 110 = 100 + 10$

$\left(\quad \right)^2 \quad 121 = 100 + 10 + 10 + 1$

$3 \quad 131 = 100 + 10 + 10 + 10 + 1$

Where:

A = the future value of the investment/loan, including interest
P = the principal investment amount (the initial deposit or loan amount)
r = the annual interest rate (decimal)
n = the number of times that interest is compounded per year
t = the number of years the money is invested or borrowed for

Note that this formula gives you the future value of an investment or loan, which is compound interest **plus** the principal. Should you wish to calculate the compound interest only, you need this:

Total compounded interest = $P(1 + r/n)^{(nt)} - P$

Two Investors Example - 10% Compound Interest

	INDIVIDUAL A			INDIVIDUAL B	
AGE	ANNUAL PAYMENT	ACCUMULATION END OF YEAR	AGE	ANNUAL PAYMENT	ACCUMULATION AT END OF YEAR
22	$4000	$4,420	22	0	
23	$4000	$9,300	23	0	
24	$4000	$14,690	24	0	
25	$4000	$20,650	25	0	
26	$4000	$27,230	26	0	
27	$4000	$34,500	27	0	
28	$4000	$42,530	28	0	
29	0	$46,990	29	$4000	$4,420
39	0	$127,200	39	$4000	$84,000
49	0	$344,330	49	$4000	$299,420
59	0	$932,110	59	$4000	$882,590
62	0	$1,256,660	62	$4000	$1,204,580
TOTAL CONTRIBUTIONS	$28,000			$136,000	
TOTAL ACCUMULATION AT AGE 62	$1,256,660			$1,204,580	

Let's look at an example
NOTE: TIME is what made the difference in accumulating more money because compound interest could do its magic even when the younger person stopped contributing funds after a deposit of $28,000.

START NOW if you are between 18-33!!!

That doesn't mean that anyone over 33 shouldn't save or invest. It is time if you haven't started.

[Source: http://www.thecalculatorsite.com/articles/finance/compound-interest-formula.php]

(3) Rule of 72

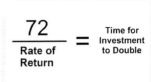

The rule of 72 is a shortcut to estimate the number of years required to double your money at a given annual rate of return. The rule states that you divide the rate, expressed as a percentage, into 72:

Years required to double investment = 72 ÷ compound annual interest rate

Note that a compound annual return of 8% is plugged into this equation as 8, not 0.08, giving a result of 9 years (not 900).

BREAKING DOWN 'Rule Of 72'

The rule of 72 is a useful shortcut, since the equations related to compound interest are too complicated for most people to do without a calculator. To find out exactly how long it would take to double an investment that returns 8% annually, one would have to use this equation:

$$T = \ln(2)/\ln(1.08) = 9.006$$

9

Most people cannot do logarithmic functions in their heads, but they can do 72 ÷ 8 and get almost the same result. Conveniently, 72 is divisible by 2, 3, 4, 6, 8, 9, and 12, making the calculation even simpler.

The rule can also be used to find the amount of time it takes for money's value to halve due to inflation. If inflation is 6%, then a given amount of money will be worth half as much in 72 ÷ 6 = 12 years. Nor does the unit have to be money: the rule could apply to population, for example.

Adjusting For Higher Rates

The rule of 72 is reasonably accurate for interest rates between 6% and 10%. When dealing with rates outside this range, the rule can be adjusted by adding or subtracting 1 from 72 for every 3 points the interest rate diverges from 8%. So for 11% annual compounding interest, the rule of 73 is more appropriate; for 14%, it would be the rule of 74; for 5%, the rule of 71.

For example, say you have a 22% rate of return (congratulations). The rule of 72 says the initial investment will double in 3.27 years. Since 22 − 8 is 14, and 14 ÷ 3 is 4.67 ≈ 5, the adjusted rule would use 72 + 5 = 77 for the numerator. This gives a return of 3.5, meaning you'll have to wait another quarter to double your money. The period given by the logarithmic equation is 3.49, so the adjusted rule is more accurate.

Adjusting For Continuous Compounding

For daily or continuous compounding, using 69.3 in the numerator gives a more accurate result. Some people adjust this to 69 or 70 for simplicity's sake.

[source: http://www.investopedia.com/terms/r/ruleof72.asp#ixzz4ZqWhiu5W]

(4) Return on Investment

Measures the gain or loss generated on an investment relative to the amount of money invested. ROI is usually expressed as a percentage and is typically used for personal financial decisions, to compare a company's profitability or to compare the efficiency of different investments.

- ### The return on investment formula is:

ROI = (Net Profit / Cost of Investment) x 100

How it works (Example):
The ROI calculation is flexible and can be manipulated for different uses. A company may use the calculation to compare the ROI on different potential investments, while an investor could use it to calculate a return on a stock.

For example, an investor buys $1,000 worth of stocks and sells the shares two years later for $1,200. The net profit from the investment would be $200 and the ROI would be calculated as follows:

ROI = (200 / 1,000) x 100 = 20%

The ROI in the example above would be **20%**. The calculation can be altered by deducting taxes and fees to get a more accurate picture of the total ROI.

The same calculation can be used to calculate an investment made by a company. However, the calculation is more complex because there are more inputs. For example, to figure out the net profit of an investment, a company would need to track exactly how much cash went into the project and the time spent by employees working on it.

Why it Matters:
ROI is one of the most used profitability ratios because of its flexibility. That being said, one of the downsides of the ROI calculation is that it can be manipulated, so results may vary between users. When using ROI to compare investments, it's important to **use the same inputs** to get an accurate comparison.

Also, it's important to note that the basic ROI calculation does not take time into consideration. Obviously, it's more desirable to get a +15% return over one year than it is over two years
[Source: http://www.investinganswers.com/financial-dictionary/technical-analysis/return-investment-roi-1100]

Top 5 Best Online Savings Accounts: February 2017

The best online savings accounts pay a good interest rate, are fully secured, and allow for flexibility. Find the best high interest savings accounts to consider.
Saving money is one of the smartest financial practices to have, but did you know that there's a, shall we say, dumb way of doing it?

Interest rates on the typical bank savings accounts are laughably low - the average national interest rate was only 0.06% as of October 17, 2016. Now, I spent years parking my hard-earned savings in that typical savings account you get with a bank checking account. And guess what? My savings just pretty much sat there, doing nothing. I didn't know any better. The $10 a year I was getting in interest was a joke.

And then I caught on that I could be earning a LOT more in interest with online savings account options that **pay over 10x the national interest rate**. Why not let your hard-earned savings work for you instead of just sitting there?

So I'm going to share my research and go over the **top 5 online high yield savings accounts**. Don't make my mistake (I'm still mad about all the interest I could have earned over the years) and use one of these to get the most out of your savings.

What to Look for in a Savings Account

Before we get into the recommendations, there are a few things you absolutely want to have in an online savings account:

1. **Security**. My big hesitation was whether it's safe to store my money with someone else. No worries - the ones on this list are all FDIC insured, which means that if the bank defaults, the government will pay you back everything you had in the account (up to $250,000).
2. **Flexibility**. Of course, you want to be able to remove your money at any time when you need to use it, without penalty. All of these allow you to transfer money to your existing checking account at any time.
   Note: Note that federal regulation limits how many times you can take your money out - you can make only 6 ACH withdrawals/transfers from a savings account per statement cycle. Also know that it may take a few days for electronic transfers to complete.
3. **Yield rate**. After I'm sure my money is secure and that I can access it, really, all I care about is the interest rate. It's pretty obvious that you want the highest interest rate you can get.

But one thing to beware of: some accounts have a **minimum balance requirement**. If you don't maintain that balance, you'll have to pay a monthly fee. If you're just parking your money there (which is the purpose of a savings account), then this shouldn't be a problem. But to be fair, I'm including options with no account minimums as well.

Tip: Some online savings accounts give you extras like ATM access and bill pay. While these features are nice, you're probably already able to do those with your current bank account. So to me, it's not an important feature. But if these are important activities for you, do some further research to see which accounts below have those features.

Best Online Savings Accounts

Here are the top 5 online savings accounts with high yields. Note: Information including interest rates, benefits and fees were obtained on October 20, 2016 from published websites and are believed to be accurate, but not guaranteed.

Best Savings with Highest Interest: Popular Direct

POPULAR |DIRECT| 1.15%, $5,000 minimum deposit:
(1) The Popular Direct Savings Account is through Banco Popular North America (BPNA), a New York State chartered bank. It currently offers **one of the highest rates at 1.15%**.
The downside is that the **minimum deposit is a whopping $5,000**. And you must maintain a **$500 balance** in the account or else you'll be charged a $4 monthly fee. If you close the account within 180 days, there's an early closing fee of $25.

Best Savings with ATM Card: Synchrony Bank

 1.05%, $0 minimum deposit:
(2) Synchrony (which used to be part of General Electric) **doesn't require a minimum deposit or a minimum balance**. And there's no monthly service fee. So this makes a solid choice for those who are just starting to save. The APY rate is a respectable **1.05%**.

Another great feature with Synchrony is that **it comes with an ATM card**, so you can withdraw savings quickly (up to 6 per statement cycle) instead of having to wait a few days for the transfer to be completed.

Best Savings for Young Adults to Open: Salem Five Direct

SalemFivedirect   1.10%, $100 minimum deposit:

(3) If you have **$100 to start with**, Salem Five Direct (the online branch of Salem Five Cents Savings Bank based in Massachusetts) offers a **slightly higher APY at 1.10%** (for balances up to $500,000). There is **no minimum balance requirement** and no monthly fees. Although you might not have heard of this bank, it's actually got a long banking history of over 160 years.

Did you know: Salem Five Direct also offers an eOne Combo option, where you can pair it with their checking account. The checking account has no minimum balance and a yield of 0.25% APY. Salem Five Direct never charges an ATM fee and will reimburse fees by other banks up to $15 per statement cycle.

Best Customer Service: Ally Bank

ally   1.00%, $0 minimum deposit:

(4) Founded in 1919, **Ally Bank** was previously General Motors Acceptance Corp. (GMAC), so it's got a pretty solid history. There is **no minimum deposit** required to open an account (but you must fund it within 30 days of account opening) and there is no monthly service fee. The rate is lower at **1.00% APY**, but many people love Ally Bank for its incredibly **user-friendly site** and **great customer service**. A real human is available to help 24/7.

Best High Yield Money Market: EverBank Yield Pledge

EverBank   1.11%, $1,500 minimum deposit:

(5) This last one isn't technically a savings account, but rather a high yield money market account. But for this article, both pretty much serve the same purpose. You can also make up to 6 withdrawals/transfers per statement cycle. Everbank gives you a **first year introductory APY of 1.11%** for balances up to $250,000. After that, the ongoing APY is currently 0.61%. Everbank promises that the yield of your account will stay in the **top 5%** of similar accounts offered in the U.S. banking market.

You also get **ATM access and a debit card**, so you have easier access to your money. Everbank never charges an ATM fee. And if you have over $5,000 in the account, Everbank will even reimburse 100% of the ATM fees charged by other U.S. banks. **Did you know:** Everbank also offers a Yield Pledge checking account with an introductory APY of 1.11% for the first year, and 0.25%-0.61% after that, depending on your balance. Pretty awesome for a checking account.

Why Open a Savings Account

The purpose of a savings account is to have **somewhere secure to park money that you may need to use in the near future**. Such as for a down payment for a house, for a big vacation, or for family planning. The reason why you want to put this kind of money in a separate account from your checking is because you don't want to accidentally spend it.

Because you may need to use this money at any time, you want an account that **lets you transfer the money out without penalty or fees**. This is the advantage of a savings account, as opposed to an investment account like a Roth IRA. Even though investment accounts may offer higher returns for your money, you may be penalized and take a tax hit if you try to take out the money early.

Tip: The best thing to do is to have enough in your checking account for everyday needs, and put money in savings for emergencies and any upcoming goals. After that, if you can, put money you don't need in the near-future in investments for long-term goals and retirement planning.

A high yield savings account is a **surefire way to grow your money a little**, but remember, it's not an investment account so you're not going to get rich off of it. And it's also not a checking account, so don't set one up if you need to make a ton of withdrawals.

Is an Online Saving Account Right for You?

Before you stash your money into one of the above savings accounts, here are some things to consider:

- **Do you need quick access to your money?** Remember, a savings account's purpose is to SAVE money, not spend it. So an online savings account doesn't make it easy for you to get at your money. If you want to make a withdrawal (like transferring money out to your bank account), it often takes 3 days or more before the transfer goes through. And you typically can only make 6 withdrawals a month.
- **Are you comfortable with web banking?** Completely web-based banking means that there's no physical location where you can just stroll in and ask questions, make a deposit, withdraw money, etc. You also lose having a relationship with your local bank. Online banks do have customer support by phone (and many by web chat), but we all know how frustrating phone calls to banks can be.
- **What is your financial situation?** Think about what your goals are and your personal financial situation. If your situation is tight and you don't have a lot of spare cash at the end of every month, it may not be worth it to open another bank account just to keep a small amount of money in. Keep in mind that like traditional savings accounts, online savings accounts will have restrictions such as minimum deposit, minimum balance, and limits on withdrawals.

There Are Other Options Too

If you're not sure if a savings account is for you, some other options include:

- A **money market account**, which acts like a savings account, but gives you freer access to your money. You'll get a debit card, ATM access, and check writing abilities. But the interest rate may be lower. As we noted, Everbank provides a money market account with a high interest earning potential.
- A **CD (Certificate of Deposit)** is for longer term savings. It may give you higher rates, but there are limitations on when you can take out the money (such as a 2-year CD, 5-year CD, etc.). And you'll often need a larger deposit to open a CD account.
- A **higher yield checking account** if you need quick and frequent access to your money. It'll give you the flexibility to access your money any time you need with no restrictions. Most checking accounts don't give you any interest, but Everbank and Salem Five Direct both offer checking accounts with 0.25% APY (Everbank has a tiered system where the APY increases with a higher balance).

Common Questions
- What is an APY?
  Let's do the complicated answer first: APY stands for Annual Percentage Yield, which is the return you get over a 1-year period based on the interest rate and compounded interest (which means that your interest earns interest), and also based on the assumption that the funds will remain in the account for 1 year. The simple answer is that, basically, 1.00% APY means 1% interest.
- How are these online savings accounts able to offer such a high interest rate?
  Online banks don't have physical locations, which means that they have much lower operating costs than brick-and-mortar banks. This means they can save on overhead and pass those savings onto customers by offering better rates.
- Is my money safe in an online savings account?
  As long as you pick one that is FDIC insured, then yes. This means that if the bank defaults, the U.S. government will pay you back every cent you had in the account, up to the FDIC maximum of $250,000. All the savings accounts in this list are FDIC insured.

- Can I take my money out whenever I need to?
  Federal regulation only allows you to make 6 withdrawals/transfers per statement cycle, before a fee kicks in.
- What kind of withdrawals can I make?
  There are 4 types of withdrawals you can make: online funds transfer (like to your own bank checking account), outgoing wire transfer, telephone transfer, and check request.
- How do I make deposits?
  You can transfer money from your own bank account, send a wire transfer, or send a check. A lot of online banks (like all the ones on this list) have mobile banking too, where you can deposit checks by taking a picture of it with your phone.
- Bottom Line
  A high-interest savings account is a great way to make your money grow a little bit. Not putting your savings into one is literally like leaving money on the table. I wish I'd known that sooner. But I hope you're all the wiser now and will consider it if you're still keeping your money in an account with non-existent interest.

[*source: https://www.creditdonkey.com/online-savings-account.html*]

For Investments such as Stocks, Annuities, Roth IRAs, IRAs, 403B, 401K, Mutual Funds, Bonds, Real Estate, Collections, please seek the counsel of a financial planner. Be cautious of random administrative fees. Find someone that comes with good solid references. Do your homework and research the types of investments that exist today. Although, we are unable to recommend any one company. Look for ratings from "**A.M. Best**" and "**Fitch**" to make sure they are reputable. There are Christian Companies. Look for longevity in the financial services industry and for a solid rating from www.ethisphere.com Above all, start investing and saving as soon as possible. Go to www.advisoryhq.com to find out about the top 10 Investment Companies listed below:

Investment Companies	Websites
Betterment	https://www.betterment.com/
BlackRock	https://www.blackrock.com/
BNY Mellon Investment Management	https://www.bnymellon.com
Fidelity Investments	https://www.fidelity.com/
J.P. Morgan Asset Management	https://www.jpmorgan.com
Northern Trust Asset Management	https://www.northerntrust.com
PIMCO	https://www.pimco.com
State Street Global Advisors	https://www.ssga.com
T. Rowe Price	https://www3.troweprice.com
Vanguard	https://investor.vanguard.com

(1)   What was Oskar's attitude towards the Polish Jews that he saved?
(2)   What do you think he was feeling when he was presented with the engraved ring?
(3)   Why was Oskar Schlindler so upset over not selling his car?
(4)   If you have the time, watch the entire movie.
Use your Journal to record these thoughts

Post It Activity

❖   Write a Post-It note for every change you will make to start saving
❖   Write a Post-It note for every change you will make to start investing
❖   Write a Post-It note for every priceless investment you have in your house
❖   Write a Post-IT note for how you will start investing in kingdom minded assets
❖   Stick these on your refrigerator to remind you of your commitments

---

Today I found out what happened to billionaire Howard Hughes' money when he died.

Over his lifetime, Howard Hughes' wallet became one of the fattest of his time. It isn't known exactly how much he was worth at the time of his death, but ten years before he died, he was forced to sell his shares in the airline company TWA. The payout? $546 million (about $3.8 billion today), estimated by some to have been about 1/3 of his net worth.

When he died, there was one major problem: Hughes had no direct descendants or immediate family, and he didn't leave behind a will. At least, that's what authorities were forced to conclude after an extensive search for one. After contacting his various banks, lawyers, and employees, every hotel he'd ever stayed in, posting classifieds in various newspapers, and even consulting a psychic, they were forced to accept that settling the massive estate was not going to be an easy matter.

So just where did all of that money go after his death?

Most assumed he wanted the money to go to the Howard Hughes Medical Institute. It was well-known that he didn't want the money falling into the hands of any distant relatives, but without hard evidence, distant cousins and others began snatching for the cash.

A battle ensued between the temporary administrator of the Hughes estate, cousin and lawyer William Lummis, and those who ran the Medical Institute. It was a multi-state war, with Nevada, California, and Texas all claiming to be responsible for the distribution of the state, and all of which had their own laws about inheritance.

While the various parties were fighting it out, a couple of different wills surfaced, though eventually thrown out as fakes. A notable one was the three-page document that declared Melvin

Dummar, a gas station attendant, was to inherit 1/16 of Hughes' fortune. Supposedly, Dummar once picked Hughes up off the side of the road and gave him a ride to his hotel, and Hughes was so grateful that he left Dummar a huge chunk of money. In 1978, the will was thrown out as a forgery.

Next, "wives" started emerging from Hughes' past, taking advantage of his reclusive reputation to explain why no one had heard of them before. Terry Moore, an actress, claimed to have married Hughes twice, but provided no documentation to support her assertions. She did, in fact, once live with Hughes in the 1940s, but her claim that they were not only married, but never divorced, was called into question given the fact that she married three times after her supposed marriage to Hughes. Nevertheless, she must have put forward a good argument, or at least pestered the estate managers so much that they decided to pay her just to get rid of her, because she was paid $400,000 by the estate. Later, Moore wrote a book titled *Beauty and a Billionaire* which made the bestseller list, likely lining her pockets a bit more.

In addition to supposed wives, an extraordinary number of Hughes' supposed children decided to acknowledge their deceased father. One was said to be the lovechild of Hughes and Amelia Earhart—product of the Mile High Club?—even though Earhart never had any children. At least two were black, but their claims were thrown out as Hughes was known to be quite the racist.

You cannot get through a single day without having an impact on the world around you. What you do makes a difference, and you have to decide what kind of difference you want to make.
- Jane Goodall

After years of struggle trying to sort the people with legitimate claims from the fakers who were in it to try to grab some of the cash, a lot of the money did end up going to the Howard Hughes Medical Institute. However, a huge chunk of it also went to various Hughes heirs. According to the Wall Street Journal, around 1000 people have benefited from the estate, including 200 of Hughes' distant relatives. After liquefying many of his assets, they collectively were awarded about $1.5 billion.

Interestingly, the liquidation of the estate wasn't completely finalized until 2010—34 years after his death. The last piece of the puzzle was the Summerlin residential development. In 1996, Rouse Co. (now General Growth) agreed to buy the Summerlin land from the Hughes' estate on a 14-year repayment plan. With that, finally, the estate of Howard Hughes was laid to rest.

[Source: http://www.todayifoundout.com/index.php/2013/09/happened-howard-hughes-money-died/]

If you don't have a will created yet, it doesn't matter how old or young you are. There are online inexpensive options to get a will created. www.legalzoom.com, Error! Hyperlink reference not valid. www.lawdepot.com, *are just a few. Go to Google and search specifically for your State of Residence because the law differs from state to state. Or you can elect to hire a lawyer that specializes in writing wills. Another consideration that the Bible instructs is about inheritance. Even though, parents are to leave a material inheritance to their children, be cautious to only assign it legally when you feel they are responsible enough to handle it.*

[Proverbs 20:21, Galatians 4:1-2, 1 Cor. 12:14]

8   Bitter or Better?

In the book of Ecclesiastes, The Bible tells us that we will have every season under the sun in this life. "Valleys" of Desperation, "Mountaintops" of Victory, "Sacred" moments of Bliss, "Heartbroken" desolation of Grief, "Building" up, "Tearing" down, ... "Refraining" or "Letting Go", "Reconciliation" or "Walking away", yes, there is nothing under the sun that is not covered between the covers of the wisest book, the Divinely, Breathed and Holy inspired "Word of God".

We are told in John 16:33 that we will have troubles in this life, but don't worry because Jesus has overcome the world! That includes all its troubles. He came to earth incarnate [as a man] to experience every pain, challenge, trial and tribulation that we experience. Jesus cried. [John 11:35] .He was betrayed by close friends [John 13:21] He grew tired and experienced thirst [John 4:6-7] He even became so angry that He took a whip to some street vendors to remove them from the [outer court] temple in Jerusalem who was trying to profit in His Father's House. [John 2:13-22]   His last human experience we won't have to encounter, because no matter the degree of our sorrows it will never equal the sacrifice of His cup. His slow, methodical, and torturous death nailed to a cross between two common thieves. An act of Reconciliation to anyone that will follow Him with Heart, Soul and Mind. So, there is a resolve for all this adversity.

SUFFERINGS

Romans 5:3-5   Amplified Bible (AMP)

3 And not only *this*, but [with joy] let us exult in our sufferings *and* rejoice in our hardships, knowing that hardship (distress, pressure, trouble) produces patient endurance; 4 and endurance, proven character (spiritual maturity); and proven character, hope *and* confident assurance [of eternal salvation]. 5 Such hope [in God's promises] never disappoints *us*, because God's love has been abundantly poured out within our hearts through the Holy Spirit who was given to us.

As stated so eloquently in Roman 5:3-5, the ultimate purpose for all these trials are to mature spiritually and naturally to mirror the character of Christ. We are to follow in His footsteps towards a 'sanctified' daily life of surrender to live Holy lives, set apart [different than the culture], and presenting love letters to the world by our speech and deeds [2 Cor. 3:3] . When you entered into a covenant with the all-powerful God of the Universe, you agreed to the following ... "to take up His Cross and Follow Him"... that includes suffering, yet with a quiet confidence that He will never forsake or leave us. [Matthew 16:24-26]

As Christians, if we read and meditate on His word we come to the realization that trials are to be expected. Yet, we groan, grumble and oftentimes, ask the question "why" is this happening to me? Since, our culture creates this 'system of performance' to extend self-worth, it is no wonder why we think we are falling short. Well, "news *flash*" *WE ARE* , because that is exactly what the word 'sin' means in Hebrew...'missing the mark' However, partnered with "Grace" or unmerited favor from the Lord, that should give us hope rather than a *performance meter* to reflect our spiritual identity and growth. . So, when it really comes down to trials, how do we reset our perspective on expectations in our faith walk? How do we stay balanced in lieu of a job loss, catastrophic loss, illness, financial challenges and a myriad of other issues that can visit us at any given season.

"Expectations"

ex•pect•ant [adjective]   "Having or showing an excited feeling that something is about to happen, especially something pleasant and interesting." [Webster: source]

> *"What messes us up the most in life is the picture in our head of how it is supposed to be.*
> *-anonymous*

Quoting the First Lady of Victory Christian Church, in Middlefield, Ct., Pastor Debbie Leal, *"I have noticed over the years that most problems, conflicts", offenses, or disappointments can be traced back to an* **"unmet expectation".**

Let's explore how the Apostle Paul and his traveling companions dealt with being literally in the eye of storm to draw some conclusions on godly behavior instead of natural reactions in

Acts 27: [Please read entire chapter]

Paul and some other *fellow* prisoners are taken aboard a ship headed for Rome. It is a wonderful *'faith'* illustration because it clearly defines the difference between **'unmet expectations'** and instead being **"expectant"** in the Lord, His Word, and His sovereignty in any life circumstance.

➤ Main points from the hurricane and shipwreck [representing any challenging season]; Paul gives COUNSEL as the Godly shepherd which falls on deaf ears *[v10-11]*;

➤ Fear filled the men frequently which prompted them to *take matters* into their *own might* [natural reaction when we don't trust God] which multiplied trials *[v.17,18]*;

➤ When all their **hope** of surviving had been extinguished, **lost** and despaired *[v.20]*, the Godly shepherd **SHARES** his **FAITH** after **INTERCESSORY PRAYER** that this is all *God's intended plan* and even though the vessel [or season ends] will be destroyed, no man shall lose his life *[v 22-25]*;

➤ The Godly shepherd **WARNED/REBUKED** in bottom-line terms to those that tried escaping the ship that they would lose their lives *[v.30-32]* [John 12:25];

➤ As hope diminishes, so does the natural will to live, so the Godly shepherd **ENCOURAGES** them to eat and as a leader;

➤ Sets the **EXAMPLE and PRAISES GOD**, but sustains balance in all matters *[v. 33-36]*;

➤ With renewed strength by **HEEDING** the **TEACHINGS** of the Godly shepherd they were able to throw grain overboard [promoting maturity and shedding old self];

➤ As new mercies unfolded the next morning, a sandy beach v. rocky terrain served as an desirous exodus from the sea to ground ending this tumultuous journey [faith season];

➤ Prophetically, as the Godly shepherd had **FORETOLD** the men, the ship was destroyed but all the men's lives were spared. *[v. 40-44]*;

➤ The Godly shepherd possessed **SACRIFICIAL** love.

S o, as the progression of this story goes: "Unmet Expectations" directed them to Divine Expectation, which commanded Hope, *Hope* developed into Trust and ultimately, *Trust* manifested into "life-saving" Faith. This is important to understand from the perspective of the role of Paul or alike our Godly shepherds, Pastors around the world. .If you just extract the words above that are all in CAPS, those are the specific functions of the pastoral office. And yet, we often hold our shepherds to a supernatural standard that no human can ever be 'expected' to operate. In a manner of speaking we have just made them and any other shepherd we lean on for voids, answers and fixes an IDOL without realizing it.

Below is a comparison of how expectation can turn into idolatry :

"EXPECTATION" [IDOLTRY]	"EXPECTANCY" [FAITH IN THE LORD]
Praying to God that HE change your Situation	Praying for God's Will [His way, not yours]
Believing God will change or remove "it" that is causing you pain/discomfort [people/health]	Claiming in the Name of Jesus that the 'its' in life are to strengthen you physically, emotionally and spiritually
Placing faith in 'what' God will Do	Placing Faith in HIM
Your Attitude goes from Contentment to Bitterness, anger & ultimately self-help	Your attitude stays 'steadfast' in the hope of Our Anchor, the Lord

Study Scriptures:

(1) Acts 27   Have you ever been in the 'eye of the storm' [serious crisis emotionally, physically, financially, spiritually or all the above]?

  ❖ What was the first thing you did?

  ❖ Who did you seek counsel? Were they able to comfort you? How did praying help where friends couldn't?

  ❖ Name the top thing you did wrong during your crisis and the outcome.

resistid
✓ _al enemigo, y de nosotros huira._

(2) 1 Thess. 5:16-18, James 1:2-4, 1 Peter 5:6-10; Eph. 6:10-20 - How do we maintain the right attitude
in the middle of a crisis?

do not quench the spirit

- _pray without ceasing_
- _give thanks in everything_
- _rejoice_
- _Be patience_
- _Cast all your care upon God_
- _Be sober, be vigilant_

(3) Job 1:8-21, Genesis 37: 23-28, 2 Cor. 11:23-27 - Were these men ungodly or bring on the crisis
because of sin? Explain why or why not? Did they have expectations? How about their friends?.
What common quality did these men have? What common weakness? _They were afriend_

(4) 2 Cor. 12:7-10 -Are there trials in life where you don't get the outcome or answer you are
seeking? Why do you think the Lord allows long-suffering?

(5) Deut. 6:5-9; Prov. 22:6: Eph. 6:4 - How can we teach our children these principles? What is the
strongest way to get them to follow God's word from an early age?

Let's Get Practical - Financial Crisis Next Steps

There are so many non-profits, social programs and organizations that help in the following areas,
however, you should seek help as soon as you realize you are experiencing some life stresses. One
problem that we have seen frequently in trying to counsel people is that they WAIT too long before
seeking help. Yes, the Lord can cover you; He is a "Miracle Worker however, you need to do your part
too and reach out for help. There are many social programs that your tax dollars pay for, so you
shouldn't feel embarressed or guilty to tap into those services. This ministry offers one on one
counseling that is totally confidential and could point you to the appropriate services. Just see one of
the leaders after class or call the church office to get an appointment scheduled.

(1) <u>Serious Health Issue/Accident</u> that reduces income and generates a lot of debt -This is normally
one of the top reasons that people encounter a serous financial setback, because unexpected
life threatening injuries that can take months or even years to recover or a debilitating sickness
such as cancer.

(2) **Job Loss** - Unemployment that creates stress and possibly debt/unpaid bills -[State Labor Department to start collecting Unemployment, Job Fairs, Go back to School/Grant Money Available, start applying, freshen up your resume, etc ... get back on the horse or if you can afford it, make a career change]

(3) **Divorce** - can be catestrophic financially as well as emotionally/physically -[If the marriage absolutely can not be salvaged, then seek an amicable method to reach consensus so at minimum children don't come in between the 'emotional upheaval' and a fair way to divide the assets. Obviously, whoever becomes the primary caretaker of the children would require child support to help with the expenses. Since this is a Christian Study, counseling should be the first step so differences can be resolved. Marriage is sacred, so it should be saved.]

(4) **Taking care of Elderly Family Members** - [https://aoa.acl.gov/AoA_Programs/HCLTC/Caregiver/] ;[*https://www.eldercaredirectory.org/state-resources.htm*]

(5) **Death of a Spouse** - Since income is normally an issue here, ask family or friends to help you back on your feet. Take time out to grieve and then whenever it is appropriate for you ... rediscover this new chapter in your life. It may mean a new home, new job, or reentering the work force or just volunteering. Life wont be the same. Seek to start something new that will aid in your healing.

(6) **Death of a child** -Same as above, but oftentimes, this is a bit harder to get back to reality, so seek counseling and give yourself the time you need to grieve. Simplify life.

(7) **Bankruptcy** - [www.uscourts.gov]

(8) **Foreclosure on Home** - State & Federal Based Assistance to help you navigate [normally takes 6 months to a year or more of being behind in payments **[www.hud.gov]**

(9) **Homelessness** [Fire, Supernatural Disaster] Red Cross,Dial **211** Community Social Services.

(10) **Car Totaled or Major Repairs -** until you can pay cash, see if you can share a ride, take other transportation [bus, ride a bike, walk]. This one is why you always need an emergency fund for asset replacement or repair. Ie...household assets like washer/dryer, furnace, Air Conditioner,etc.

How to Create a Crisis Budget:

Identify only those Essential Needs that your Budget has to Contain:
- ➤ **Rent or Mortgage** - Decide early on how many months you can afford to live in the same place, seek a cheaper place as soon as you think you will get behind, live with family, friends temporarily until you are employed again, get a roommate.
- ➤ **Food** - Apply for Food Stamps if needed, Go to Community Food Banks, Soup Kitchens, Coops
- ➤ **Clothing** [essentials] - Normally just for children that are outgrowing their clothes, go to consignment shops, ask for hand-me-downs from friends/family; let people know of your situation

- ➤ **Medicine** [if life threatening disease] - Most physicians will give out samples until you can get your medications refilled or go straight to the drug manufacturer - many offer programs for low income or those in distress financially; many offer mail order discounts.
- ➤ **Health Insurance** - COBRA is always an option, but normally very expensive for someone that has just lost their job, so go to the State Department of Insurance for options of insurance coverage. State programs like Medicaid are income based and there are free programs for children that qualify.
- ➤ A **Crisis Budget should be for 3-9 months minimum**; this is why it is critical to have a diversified distribution of assets that equal cash, like savings, stocks, collections, you can sell or redeem during seasons of financial duress.
- ➤ **Work with Creditors** - Call your creditors right away and start working with them to reduce payments temporarily until you are reemployed. Most will work with you as long as you send a partial payment in and you don't disappear. Do NOT AVOID your creditors.
- ➤ **Hospital or Medical Debt** - Every year, they write off thousands of dollars of debt for those that are truly struggling with a financial issue that is longer term. However, again you need to work with them continually.

Go to YouTube and Listen to the Following Songs: "Eye of the Storm" by Ryan Stevenson; "Blessings" by Laura Story and "Trust in You" by Lauren Daigle

(1)   What is the common thread in all these songs?
(2)   Cite at least 3 Scriptures that support the lyrics.
(3)   Do you have a favorite life verse now when trials are pressing?
Use your Journal to record these thoughts

Post It Activity

Marshall Law [Military Governing] has taken over your city and they have been going house to house and arresting those that are not of the Christian Faith:
- ❖ Write a Post-It to every item in your house that shows evidence that you are a Christian
- ❖ Write a Post-It Note for every Verse you could cite by memory to the officers
- ❖ Write a Post-It Note for how you would express your faith if there weren't a lot of items representing Christianity in your home

The Ultimate Trial

"You never know how much you really believe anything until its truth of falsehood becomes a matter of life and death to you. It is easy to say you believe a rope to be strong and sound as long as you are merely using it to cord a box. But suppose you had to hang by that rope over a precipice. Wouldn't you then first discover how much you really trusted it?"

— **C.S. Lewis**, **A Grief Observed**

On November 19th, 2013, a crisp fall day, our family dynamic was suddenly and eternally changed with one heartbeat stopping abruptly. Alone. On a stretch of highway early on an otherwise ordinary Tuesday. This bright and energetic soul would've already ascended to the arms of His heavenly Father before mom would get that 'visit' from the highway patrol. As two officers stood in my doorway, I was oblivious to the news that was about to shake my world forever. Nothing prepares you for Heaven's calling on your children. It is out of order. It never makes sense. You just resign to waiting for answers. Eventually. And as you wait, the sweet memories start to let light in where darkness once paralyzed you in grief. Our son, Gabriel Nathan Miller, at 24 years young, was a budding photographer, full of life, and such an incredible light in the lives of so many. His twin brother, Jacob, while preparing for the "homecoming celebration' found the following on Gabe's computer. We are sharing this because we feel it will encourage many to keep 'fighting the good fight'.

The "LIMP"

You will lose someone you can't live without, and your heart will be badly broken, and the bad news is that you never completely get over the loss of your beloved. But this is also the good news. They live forever in your broken heart that doesn't seal back up. And you come through. It's like having a broken leg that never heals perfectly—that still hurts when the weather gets cold, but you learn to dance with the limp.

Anne Lamott

"Suffering"

By Gabe Miller

The world is constantly enticing us to do what feels good, what's easy, and ways to get the most profit from what takes the least amount of effort. It's a worldly view, a lie, this world is fallen and under the devil, and because of this we can't live a life for God and for this world. God talks about this throughout the bible. But God wants us to be strong so we don't slip into this mindset; God never said that life would be easy, although, if we put our faith in Him we can overcome any challenge. As God says in 1 Corinthians 10:13: "I will not let you be tried beyond what you can bear..." Scripture goes on to say in Romans 8:28: "That all things work together for good to them that love God..." So with this we know that even in our times of struggle that we are in the center of God's plan for our life.

We are all running a race (our life) and with that metaphor the bible says in 1 Corinthians 9:24: "...SO RUN TO WIN!..." This thought occurred to me on Monday, when I went out for a run. I was getting close to the end of the run with my brother and I felt like giving up and walking, my legs were tired, I was breathing heavy and didn't feel like running anymore. But Instead of giving up I put my head down and watched my feet, and started putting one foot in front of the other and did that till I got to our street and with the extra encouragement of not giving up, sprinted to race my brother to our drive way. Once I took the first step into my driveway I could walk, and it felt SO GOOD. I gained a lot from this experience.

One, that suffering in this life is nothing to what Hell would be, in life, we only suffer for a season and since life is so short, compared to eternity than the time we spend suffering is even less than our lives on a whole.

Two, God will cause us to suffer to strengthen us, especially in running you have to suffer to get stronger.

Three, God will never give us too much to handle, I wasn't running a marathon (like Mr. Robbins) but in my own life the suffering was hard but not too much for me to handle, through my experience things always get better right after they were the worst.

In reference to my run when I hit my drive way and started walking, it felt great for two reasons, first, that the suffering was over, and second, that I had done something that I wanted to give up on. God wants us to run to win, that means not giving up the whole way, our lives are the run and we each have different distance to the finish line but we all have the chance to win we just have to stay in shape in God to win.

So when we are suffering, we need to realize that it's not forever, only Heaven Will Be. God encouraged me with the challenges I'm going through right now and it was on my heart to share it for anyone else who is suffering.

God Bless,

Gabe

9   The Final Chapter

C heckmate? The King always has the last move....the final move ...

Ken Ulmer tells a story about two men who were in an art museum and came upon a painting of a chess game. One character looked like a man; the other character looked a lot like the Devil. The man is down to his last piece on the chessboard. The title of the painting is **"Checkmate."**

One of the two men looking at this painting was an international chess champion, and something about the painting intrigued him. He began to study it. He became so engrossed that the man with him grew impatient and asked him what he was doing. He said, "There's something about this painting that bothers me, and I want to study it for a little while. You go ahead and wander around."

Checkmate?

He studied it. His head started nodding, and his hands started moving. When his friend came back, he said, "We have to locate the man who painted this picture and tell him that either he has to change the picture, or he has to change the title."

His friend asked, "Why? What's wrong with the painting?"

The man said, "Well, it's titled '"Checkmate",' but the title is wrong. The painter's either got to change the painting or change the title, because the King still has **one more move.**"

Going down to Judea to see Lazarus would cost Jesus his life, as he knew it would. And on Good Friday, they tried him and judged him; they whipped him and beat him; they mocked him and scorned him; they hung him on a cross to die and laid him low in a tomb to rot the way every human body has rotted ever since death entered this sorry, dark world. And then they said to everybody, "That's all, folks." Show's over. Time to go home. **Checkmate.** But they were wrong, because ... **the King still had one more move!**

I don't know what challenge you face today. Maybe there is stress at work. Maybe you're in a relationship that is falling apart, or your marriage already fallen apart. Maybe there's a son or daughter, somebody that you love, who is struggling or estranged from you. Maybe you have financial pressures. Maybe you have done the wrong thing, or said the wrong thing, or made a mistake that feels so big it could never be redeemed. Maybe not. Maybe things are going pretty well, and there is no crisis at all. But there will be one day.

The mortality rate is still hovering right around 100%. Whatever you face, whether it's today or tomorrow, the promise of Jesus to everyone who puts their trust in him is this: There is **hope.** Even when it feels like "checkmate," that's not all folks, because ... **the King still has one more move.**

[Source: John Ortberg "Ultimate Hope" (sermon, 2005)]

According to the following diagram below, the wisest of financial planners will advise you to reduce your investment "risk-taking" as you grow older, especially after the age of 50. Why? Because they factor in that the median age expectancy for people in the USA, on average is 76 years old[1], so financially you don't have enough time to recover if you lose your retirement savings. Paired with increased potential of serious illness and accompanying expenses, it is considered wise to be frugal with types of investments as you age.

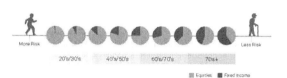

AGE APPROPRIATE INVESTING
Investment Strategies for All of Life's Seasons

More Risk   Less Risk

20's/30's   40's/50's   60's/70's   70s+

▦ Equities   ■ Fixed Income

Source: BlackRock. This is for illustrative purposes only and not indicative of any investment. This assumes your ability to change your investment allocation as you age.

[[1]source: http://www.cnbc.com/2017/02/22/us-life-expectancy-is-low-and-is-now-projected-to-be-on-par-with-mexico-by-2030.html]

However, as believers we need to grasp the understanding of what His word tells us in **Ephesians 5:13-15**; to arise out of a 'state of busy-ness, numbing 'to-and-fro' lifestyle, never considering the time fleeting by so quickly to redeem it *for* the **Lord's will**. So, review the investment strategy above again, and think about this. In **John 9:4**, "there will come a season that we no longer will be able to work, that the night is coming"...at any given time that He appoints and your legacy will be etched on the hearts of people that you touched. **Or** the dates will be etched upon a stone memorial, a funeral will be ushered quickly and life will go on as if you were merely another sunflower in the field that dropped its head and gave up its breath to the earth. Your choice. Your legacy; an accumulation of decisions you make daily for your will or **His**.

Therefore, shouldn't your primary focus be for the investment of His Kingdom, His children, and for all the LOST? Why do we get so 'tunnel-vision' in this temporary, short journey of 70-80 years [**Psalm 90:10**], that we forget that we will spend far more time in 'eternity' than here? *[not as we understand it - but as measured in God's 'out of man's perception of time]* [**2 Peter 3:8**] Therefore, every decision we make whether it is our finances, children, marriages, relationships, choices of jobs, places to live and most importantly, what we choose to do on a daily basis stitches together our unique quilt of interconnected patches of life. That life, like *no other* will determine and boldly speak to which voice we obey and ultimately nurture, feed and sustain into full maturity.

The Parable of the Two Wolves

A grandfather is talking with his grandson and he says there are two wolves inside of us which are always at war with each other.

One of them is a good wolf which represents things like kindness, bravery and love. The other is a bad wolf, which represents things like greed, hatred and fear.

The grandson stops and thinks about it for a second then he looks up at his grandfather and says, "Grandfather, which one wins?"

The grandfather quietly replies, the one you feed

There will be surprises in heaven. And regrets. Tears of joyful reunions. All-embracing final forgiveness. Complete surrender. Consecrated worship that knocks you down in adoration. Unfolding of hands pressing towards the angelic hosts. Knees free of pain to usher in leaping, dancing and frolicking with the saints of old. Quick re-runs of our lives in full 'high definition' technology that will bring us both joy and sorrow. It will be a time for reflecting, a time for wonder, a time for starting life … as only heaven appoints. A time to meet our Creator, our Personal Savior, Jesus, and to become one with His spirit. The sweetest homecoming and gathering

> "One Call from Heaven,
>
> Potentially Changes All of our Destinies"
>
> *Pastor Peter Leal, Sr. Nov. 23rd, 2013*

of one's loyal family. There will be final judgment as well as redemptive restoration. There will be a resolve so deep that manifests our souls into our true, born identity. Our thumb print of spiritual affinity will match Our Fathers'. Alas, it will be our crown's reward after suffering a short time here on earth.

Study Scriptures:

What will this life cost us? As with the great cloud of witnesses before us outlined in Hebrews, **Chapter 11**, we have been given role models that suffered. There is not one sordid trial that we encounter which even comes close to Our Savior's ultimate sacrifice of HIS liberating bloodshed. Yet, there is a "cost to the oil", the oil that anoints, sanctifies, keeps our GPS [Godly Positioning System] due North, and allows our roots to reach deep for the 'living water' that will bear up against the 'hurricanes' in this journey. [Col. 2:6-8] *Oil in the Bible most often represents the 'holy spirit'.

Let's explore some saints from scriptures which we can pull from to aid us in similar trials:

> ➤ In Genesis 22:1-12- retells the account of God instructing Abraham to take his *only* 'miracle' child, Isaac, to a mountain top and offer him up as a burnt offering. This is the first time that 'love' is used in the Bible. It signifies the depth of the love between father and son, but also the depth of trust Abraham had for HIS God. There will be a time when we all are presented with an "ISAAC" moment of truth. It will reveal our commitment to our relationship with the Lord, or shake the very foundation

22:2 whom thou lovest. It is providentially significant that this is the first occurrence of the word "love" in the Bible, referring as it does to the love of a father for his son. The New Testament makes it clear that this story of Abraham and Isaac is not only true historically but is also a type of the heavenly Father and His only begotten Son, depicting the coming sacrifice on Mount Calvary. In a beautiful design (no doubt Spirit-inspired), it is appropriate that the first use of "love in each of the three synoptic gospels (Matthew 3:17; Mark 1:11; Luke 3:22) shows the Father calling out from heaven that "this is my beloved Son," at the baptism of Jesus (which, of course, also speaks of death and resurrection). In the Gospel of John, on the other hand, where the word "love" occurs more than in any other book of the Bible, its first occurrence is at John 3:16: "God so loved the world" that He, like Abraham, was willing to sacrifice His beloved Son.

GPS Godly Positioning System.

Oil - Holy Spirit

88

of our beliefs. In order to be prepared for any treasure you grasp tightly to be loosed if the Lord wills it, commit yourself fully to ... (1) studying and meditating on the word of God, (2) worshipping and thanking Him frequently, (3) getting connected to a body of Christ [local church membership] and (4) praying without ceasing. . Therefore, **your faith will be tested beyond any natural ability to survive it so it will be by spiritual means you will walk through it victoriously.** A personal relationship with Jesus Christ and possessing a deep heart knowledge of His promises will provide the guidance.

La Viuda y los jaros de aceite.

➤ In .2 Kings 4:1-7 - Recalls the story of when a widow is confronted by creditors who has threatened to take her children as indentured slaves for repayment of debt left from her deceased husband. She is filled with fear, but she wisely seeks the counsel from the prophet Elisha. Elisha asks her to inventory her house for any assets that can repay the debt; at first she denies anything of value ... but then recalls, "yes, a bit of oil". [a common household staple] Upon that answer, Elisha instructs her to asks her neighbors and friends for as many jars to hold the oil and then sell it. The outcome is quite a miraculous witness to the village, the widow and most certainly for her young sons. She not only earns enough money to pay off the debt but she has enough to live off for the remainder of their lives. It is a testimony of what can happen if you obey the Lord's instruction and the miracles that still occur today. . **Therefore, your faith will be tested by believing in God's miraculous ways, and by 'doing' what HE instructs you to DO.** In order to do what HE instructs you to do, you should crave a deep and intimate prayer relationship with your personal Savior, Jesus Christ, yearn to hear the whisper of the Holy Spirit and the directions from your Heavenly Father. You need to learn to depend on those natural needs via supernatural means.

➤ In Esther Chapters 1-7 - Esther is named Queen of Persia after a carefully orchestrated search for the perfect virgin is enacted region wide Esther is placed in a precarious and risky position to outwit, Haman, a manipulative enemy of the Jewish people. He becomes an enemy of the Jews upon being insulted by Mordecai [Esther's uncle] , because he wouldn't pay him honor per protocol granted of high officials. Haman's pride being bruised seeks and gains approval from the King to commit a genocide of the Jewish people, claiming cultural differences too vast. Upon learning this, Mordecai becomes greatly distressed, whereas, Esther learning of his mental state sends a messenger to find out what is wrong. Esther finds out the plot against the Jews and even though, she has not been summoned to the King's court for 30 days must bravely approach him *uninvited*.[which could be a death warrant, because the king had to summon you first...no open door policy]. *So*, it is what Esther does before approaching the King that gives us insight when faced with 'action' that will be 'politically incorrect'. She requests that *all of the Jews in Susa*, *her maids* to enter into a fast of no food or drink for 3 days and 3 nights, including herself. She takes a serious **pause** for **prayer** to approach the King *uninvited*. The next day she goes to the outer court and the King accepts her invitation; she requests that she throw a banquet for the King and Haman which the King agrees to. Meanwhile, that night upon a sleepless night, King Xerxes, does some light reading of the chronicles [journals tracking behavior around the court] and discovers the potential assassination stopped by Mordecai's swift action. The King decides to honor Mordecai, so he asks Haman how he would show honor to a man. Haman thinks the King is talking about him , so suggests a public ride on one of the King's best horses, adorned in the robe of distinguished honor. How all this gets progressively gets worse for Haman, as the second day of the banquet when Queen Esther reveals that it is Haman trying to annihilate the Jewish people When the King hears this by Queen Esther, Haman is hung on the very gallows Haman had prepared for Mordecai. Alas, the Jewish people are saved. **Therefore, there will be times in your life that calls for bold, politically incorrect action that defends your loyalty to the Lord as a Believer. This should be preceded cautiously by deep communion, fasting periods to wait on His perfect timing, His words to be issued and His grace to prevail.**

> In Matt. 26:6-13 & Luke 7:47 - A woman enters into the home of Simon, a Pharisee, where Jesus was having dinner with his disciples [pretty much crashing their dinner party, but alas there is good cause]. She has recently been excused of several demons by Jesus and she has come into full realization of the love that the Lord has extended and freed her from her former life of sin.[prostitution] She is overtaken by emotion, and displays her gratefulness by pouring her expensive perfume over the head of Jesus and baptizing his feet with her tears; she was moved deeply acknowledging His lordship over her life. [perfume thought to be worth a years' salary or 300 denarii] Of course, the Pharisees in their true religious 'state of thinking' judged this behavior by stating it was a total waste of money; that this could have fed many poor people. And furthermore, asking Jesus, why he would allow a woman of the 'red light' district to touch him in such a manner? Priceless. Jesus, retorts the following in verses Mark 7:47 … you offered no foot washing when I entered your home, yet she removed the dust with her tears and wipe them dry with her hair …. you offered no welcoming but she has not stopped kissing my feet … you offered no oil upon my head yet she poured perfume liberally on my head and feet. **Therefore, there will times that the Lord breaks your flesh, your heart to take you deeper in your relationship with Him. As you are a rightful recipient of His forgiveness, grace and all-consuming love, LOVE Him with all your HEART, SOUL AND MIND. Don't ever forget your FIRST love.**

Questions:

1. What is the common theme throughout these Bible stories?

    God's love

2. When you accepted the Lord, what emotions flooded over you? Or did your life just start changing by your decisions? How did decisions in the stories affect the outcome?

3. Read Ecc. 12:13-14 ; 2 Cor. 5:9-10 - What will happen for each of us eventually?
    Judged before the Throne of God

4. Stand before the Lord in judgment for even the tiniest deed/action/word. Read 2 Cor. 4:18 - What should be our focus in this life?
   Eternity

Let's Get Practical - No One Wants to Plan This, but you Really Should

(1) **THE Funeral Rule:** Enforced by the Federal Trade Commission (FTC), makes it possible for you to choose only those goods and services you want or need and to pay only for those you select, whether you are making arrangements when a death occurs or in advance. The Rule allows you to compare prices among funeral homes, and makes it possible for you to select the funeral arrangements you want at the home you use. (The Rule does not apply to third-party sellers, such as casket and monument dealers, or to cemeteries that lack an on-site funeral home.)

Funeral Planning Tips

(1)
(2) Shop around in advance. Compare prices from at least two funeral homes. Remember that you can supply your own casket or urn.
(3) Ask for a price list. The law requires funeral homes to give you written price lists for products and services.
(4) Resist pressure to buy goods and services you don't really want or need.
(5) Avoid emotional overspending. It's not necessary to have the fanciest casket or the most elaborate funeral to properly honor a loved one.
(6) Recognize your rights. Laws regarding funerals and burials vary from state to state. It's a smart move to know which goods or services the law requires you to purchase and which are optional.
(7) Apply the same smart shopping techniques you use for other major purchases. You can cut costs by limiting the viewing to one day or one hour before the funeral, and by dressing your loved one in a favorite outfit instead of costly burial clothing.
(8) Shop in advance. It allows you to comparison shop without time constraints, creates an opportunity for family discussion, and lifts some of the burden from your family.

[*Source: https://www.consumer.ftc.gov/articles/0302-types-funerals*]

(2) **LIFE Insurance:** www.lifehappens.org is a great educational web site that helps you determine what coverage you will need for life, disability and for long term care. This study recommends only "term life insurance", but this is a personal choice. The State of Connecticut, **Department of Insurance** manages the oversight of sellers of insurance policies to ensure they are adhering to State laws.

Scenario One

You just received a phone call from the estate of a long-lost relative. You have inherited a million dollars in cash! The key to the box is in a silver container hidden at the summit of Mount McKinley in Alaska — at 20,320 feet, the tallest mountain in North America. The instructions are clear — you must personally climb the mountain (no helicopters!) and retrieve the key yourself. If you complete the task within 12 months from today, the money is yours. If not, you lose the money forever.

Explain the approach you would take to accomplish this goal

List IN ORDER , at least 10 Steps you Would take in Order to Accomplish the Goal:

Scenario Two

You have received horrible news from a State Trooper that your husband was the only fatality in a 4 car pile-up, leaving you a young widow & single parent of two children, ages 5 & 7. At your late husband's funeral, his very wealthy parents appear to serve you with legal documents demanding full custody of their two grandchildren, claiming you [their daughter-in-law] was not fit as a mother or financially stable to support them. Therefore, in order to raise enough funds [estimated at 1 million] over next 1 2 months to cover the costs of this tremendous legal battle, retain your home and pay your bills and most importantly retain custody of your children ....

Explain the approach you would take to accomplish this goal

List IN ORDER , at least 10 Steps you Would take in Order to Accomplish the Goal:

Parallelisms to Scenarios 1 & 2

Climbing Mountain: Physical Income Motivation	Saving Lives: Spiritual Income Motivation
Assess, research, plan, prepare & train for journey, hire an expert, or consultation	Who paid the biggest ransom? Why do the motivators change? Why do we get more people involved to help us?
Save or raise funds for trip, practice, adjust plans, assess health, pray, mentally prepare	Why do we set limits to 10%? Where does our citizenship reside? Why are we more concerned with the physical income?
Execute on plan, readjust, face challenges, don't give up, keep trying until you reach your goals	Strategically consider & plan for the financial goals that will promote God's Kingdom.

"Consider this...which retirement plan is more permanent...your Earthly or Heavenly one?"

What conclusions from this exercise did you discover?

(1)   Write your obituary how you would like to be remembered
(2)   Write your obituary on how you think your loved ones will remember you.
(3)   Has your perspective on your life changed?

Use your Journal to record these thoughts

Post It Activity

The Lord tells you your life will end at midnight today and tells you are forbidden to tell anyone, but you have permission to write 3 post-it notes [anything but your life is going to end]:

❖   Who was your first selected Post-it Note to? Why?
❖   Did you write anyone to seek forgiveness?
❖   What was the most important message on your post-it notes?

The Last Time

Wednesday 12 October 2016 09:55 BST

When you are in the middle of all the little things you do again and again with young children and the days are long and the nights are broken it can seem endless. This beautiful poem reminds us to hold onto the little things - as one day you will do them for the last time and when you no longer do them you will yearn for just one more day of them.

The Last Time

From the moment you hold your baby in your arms,

You will never be the same.

You might long for the person you were before,

When you had freedom and time,

And nothing in particular to worry about.

You will know tiredness like you never knew it before,

And days will run into days that are exactly the same,

Full of feeding and burping,

Whining and fighting,

Naps, or lack of naps. It might seem like a never-ending cycle.

But don't forget...

There is a last time for everything.

There will come a time when you will feed your baby for the very last time.

They will fall asleep on you after a long day

And it will be the last time you ever hold your sleeping child.

One day you will carry them on your hip,

then set them down,

And never pick them up that way again.

You will scrub their hair in the bath one night

And from that day on they will want to bathe alone.

They will hold your hand to cross the road,

Then never reach for it again.

They will creep into your room at midnight for cuddles,

And it will be the last night you ever wake for this.

One afternoon you will sing 'the wheels on the bus' and do all the actions,

Then you'll never sing that song again.

They will kiss you goodbye at the school gate,

the next day they will ask to walk to the gate alone.

You will read a final bedtime story and wipe your last dirty face.

They will one day run to you with arms raised,

for the very last time.

The thing is, you won't even know it's the last time

until there are no more times, and even then,

it will take you a while to realize.

So while you are living in these times,

remember there are only so many of them and when they are gone,

you will yearn for just one more day of them

For one last time.

Author unknown
[Source: https://www.netmums.com/child/the-last-time---poem-for-parents]

And this represents life in general. There is one last time for every season, every joy, every heartache, and eventually for this very life we hold dear and true. We get this one chance to be the sweet fragrance that fills the room with His presence, our voice to invite the lost to His almighty throne and leave our spiritual and physical imprint on the hearts of men and women. So make your first, seconds and thirds count until that last time, so there are no regrets or unreconciled relationships to mend. Make your last times count because we never know when they will occur.

However, the good news is the last time we take a breath, will launch us into an incredible first and last time packaged together for all of eternity. . .

10   A Personal Testimony

One day, a little girl is sitting and watching her mother do the dishes at the kitchen sink.

She suddenly notices that her mother has several strands of white hair sticking out in contrast on her brunette head. "Why are some of your hairs white, Mom?" she asks.

Her mother replies, "Well, every time you do something wrong and make me cry or unhappy, one of my hairs turns white."

The little girl thinks about this awhile, then asks, "So how come ALL of Grandma's hairs are white?"

Pause and think about it. Too many 'born-again' Christians are still shackled to the bondages of the past that are preventing them from realizing the full bounty of Calvary's liberties. "There exists in each of each a 'chapter' we would rather not discuss. A chapter that still takes us backwards into regret, guilt and sorrow, the tools of the devil who loves to keep us spinning on the 'wash' cycle when we have been totally cleansed by the blood of Our Redeemer, Jesus Christ."

Too many "born again" Christians have lost the luster of that fresh, anointing or passionate love they once enjoyed due to life's disappointments paralyzing them to mediocrity. A life listening to the world's reflections instead of God's promises, focusing on the perceived delays and detours as failures, and buying into the American dream of accumulating *"more"* to fill the void only Jesus can seal. So, it is time to reevaluate your commitment to 'taking up His Cross and following Him. Whether you have already accepted the Lord as your personal Savior and Lord over your life or you just haven't been ready to surrender your will for His, it is time for a lot of us to make a serious covenant with our King of Kings, Jesus Christ.

So, right where you are sitting don't waste any more time "going through the motions" like signing up for gym membership and then going twice throughout the year. Write a "love letter" to your Heavenly Father to show gratitude for the price His only begotten Son paid to set you free. This will take a commitment daily for the rest of your life, so don't hastily promise in a moment of spiritual stirring, but as written in **2 Corinthians 2:1-16** :

2 And so it was with me, brothers and sisters. When I came to you, I did not come with eloquence or human wisdom as I proclaimed to you the testimony about God. ²For I resolved to know nothing while I was with you except Jesus Christ and him crucified. ³I came to you in weakness with great fear and trembling. ⁴My message and my preaching were not with wise and persuasive words, but with a demonstration of the Spirit's power, ⁵so that your faith might not rest on human wisdom, but on God's power. God's Wisdom Revealed by the Spirit.
⁶We do, however, speak a message of wisdom among the mature, but not the wisdom of this age or of the rulers of this age, who are coming to nothing. ⁷No, we declare God's wisdom, a mystery that has been hidden and that

---

the wash cycle

"There exists in each of us a 'chapter' we would rather not discuss. A chapter that still takes us backwards into regret, guilt and sorrow, the tools of the devil who loves to keep us spinning on the 'wash' cycle when we have been totally cleansed by the blood of Our Redeemer, Jesus Christ."

God destined for our glory before time began. *8 None of the rulers of this age understood it, for if they had, they would not have crucified the Lord of glory. 9 However, as it is written:*

"What no eye has seen,
What no ear has heard, and
What no human mind has conceived"
the things God has prepared for those who love him."
— 10 these are the things God has revealed to us by his Spirit.

The Spirit searches all things, even the deep things of God. 11 For who knows a person's thoughts except their own spirit within them? In the same way no one knows the thoughts of God except the Spirit of God. 12 What we have received is not the spirit of the world, but the Spirit who is from God, so that we may understand what God has freely given us. 13 This is what we speak, not in words taught us by human wisdom but in words taught by the Spirit, explaining spiritual realities with Spirit-taught words. 14 The person without the Spirit does not accept the things that come from the Spirit of God but considers them foolishness, and cannot understand them because they are discerned only through the Spirit. 15 The person with the Spirit makes judgments about all things, but such a person is not subject to merely human judgments, 16 for,
"Who has known the mind of the Lord so as to instruct him?"
But we have the mind of Christ.
If you have never 'really' surrender your life to Jesus Christ, recite from your heart the following prayer in the privacy of your home. This isn't about collecting notches on anyone's belt of righteousness, so this is between you and the Lord. Then when you are ready to proclaim a public announcement of your faith in Christ, you can do so through water baptism, which symbolizes being born again in the triune Godhead, The Father, Son and Holy Ghost..

Father,

You loved the world so much that YOU gave your only begotten Son to die for our sins so that whosoever believes in HIM will not perish but have eternal life. [John 3:16]

YOUR WORD says we are saved by grace [Eph. 2:8] through faith as a gift from YOU. There is nothing we can do to *earn* salvation.

I believe and confess with my mouth that Jesus Christ is YOUR SON, the SAVIOR of the World. I believe that HE died on the Cross for me and bore all my sins, Paying the PRICE for them.

I believe in my heart that YOU raised Jesus from the dead and that HE is alive today.

I am a sinner and I am sorry for my sins and I ask YOU to forgive me. By faith I received Jesus Christ now as my LORD and SAVIOR. I believe that I am saved and will spend eternity with YOU.

Thank YOU, FATHER! I am so grateful! In JESUS precious name, AMEN.

If you just need a recommitment to the Lord, dust off that Bible …. Start pressing in again to devour its riches, pray without ceasing, worship HIM with abandonment, surround yourself with Godly people and above all get connected to a home church where you make a commitment to serving. This journey of 'sanctification' was never intended to be accomplished by being a 'righteous loner'; you are to have friendships whereas, "Iron sharpens Iron." Come to HIS throne with a repentant, pliable heart as instructed in Psalm 51, especially verse 17 … the only sacrifice the Lord desires is a heart that is willing to be broken for what breaks the heart of God, a penitent attitude [action is demanded to truly turn your habits around] and a gratefulness that leads to a truly transformed life.

Now, its time to write your personal testimony after taking this Bible Study for the past 9 weeks.

Answer the following questions to help navigate your own testimony: [cite scriptures to support your answers if able]

(1) What preconception/ideas did you have regarding this Bible Study when you first signed up?

What first came to my mind, was about that we were going to send a ti and of diezmos y ofrendas lot of times talking and studying what our obligation

(2) What did you end up discovering that this Bible Study was about? *are to god with our money.*

Il was more then just that. It was about about our finance but in may diferent ways. Debts

(3) What was the number ONE thing that blew your mind about what God/Bible had to say about money issues? Why? *We have to give God what belongs to him but we also have to comply with the law.*

(4) What have you taken away from the Bible Study, and how has this changed your life, marriage, spirituality and overall stewardship over all that the Lord has blessed you with?

Money is not everything in life ;

(5) Why would you recommend this Bible Study to another person? [If you won't, that is ok too!] Would you be willing to give your testimony before the Church? [Total volunteer basis]

Tax Retirement Funeral Exp.   Co-Sign

A

Accrued Interest

Accrued interest is unpaid interest that accumulates on the principal balance of a loan, adding to the total amount owed in a loan.

Additional principal payment

An additional principal payment made towards the principal balance of a loan. This can enable the borrower's future interest payments to be reduced. In amortized loans, such as most mortgages and auto loans, most of the early payments go toward principal. If you can make at least one extra payment a year, you can cut the length of a loan by as much as a quarter.

Adjustable-rate mortgage

An adjustable-rate mortgage, or ARM, is a form of financing secured by real estate which carries an interest rate that may change over the life of the loan. The interest rate on an ARM is defined as a variable financial index plus or minus a margin, such as "1-year Constant Maturity Treasury plus 2.5%."

Amortization schedule

It is a comprehensive schedule of payments tabling the break- up of the mortgage amount, interest amount, principle received, and balance due through each period of loan till the loan balances reaches nil.

Appraisal

It is an estimated value of a property, based on a analytical comparison of similar saleable property. See further Appraiser, Assessment, Fair market value

Appreciation

It is the rise in the value of property because of fluctuations in market conditions and other causes like inflation, costs and standard of living.

Asset

Any property or possession so owned by an individual that has monetary value is an asset. They include real estate, personal property and debts owed to the individual by others. Liquid assets are those which can be quickly converted into cash like bank accounts, stocks and shares, bonds, mutual funds etc.

B

Bankruptcy

It is a legally declared inability of an individual or organization to pay their creditors. Bankruptcy is filed in a Federal Court. Bankruptcies are of various types. The most common one however, is the 'Chapter 7 No Asset' bankruptcy which relieves the individual/borrower of his debts and liabilities. The borrower remains ineligible for an 'A' paper loan for a period of two years after the bankruptcy has been discharged. He is also required to re-establish the ability to repay debt.

Before-tax income

Before-tax income is the gross earnings of an individual or company prior to the deduction of taxes.

Beneficiary

A beneficiary is any individual or legal entity that's named as an inheritor of funds or property in a bank account, trust fund, insurance policy, will, or similar financial contract.

Bill of Sale

The document that concludes the transfer of new property.

Billing cycle

Billing cycle refers to the length of time that passes between statement dates. For credit cards, the billing cycle is commonly one month.

Blue Book

The Blue Book, also called Kelley Blue Book, is a printed valuation guide that assists vehicle owners, auto dealers, and insurance companies in determining the market value or sales price of a vehicle. [www.kbb.com]

Bond

A bond is a loan that's sold in shares as a security. Corporations and government entities sell bond shares to raise money for special projects, expansion, or simply to cover budgeted expenses. One who purchases a bond is called the bondholder. The terms of the bond specify when and how the bond issuer will repay the principal to the bondholder.

Book value

Book value is the cost of an item or capital asset plus the cost of additions, less depreciation. In the case of financial records, book value is the net amount attributed to an asset on a balance sheet. The term can also refer to the net worth of a company's common stock equity.

Buyer's remorse

A buyer's second thoughts after buying a house or other major purchase, a feeling of anxiety or being overwhelmed by the thought of another financial responsibility.

C

Cancellation of debt

Cancellation of debt is the writing off of a borrower's outstanding principal balance, even though payment hasn't been made. The lender essentially wipes away the debt, and the borrower is free from obligation.

Capital gain

A capital gain is the increase in an asset's value, such that it becomes worth more than the purchase price. The gain is known as an unrealized capital gain until the asset is sold. Once the asset is sold and the profit is made, the gain is called a realized capital gain.

Cardholder agreement

A cardholder agreement is the written statement of terms that governs a credit card account. The Federal Reserve requires credit card companies to provide cardholders with a cardholder agreement that defines the annual percentage rate, how minimum payments are calculated, annual account fees, and rights of the card holder when billing disagreements arise.

Cashier's check

A cashier's check is a draft written by a bank and signed by a bank cashier or officer. Cashier's checks do not bounce, as a personal check might, because the instrument is drawn on the bank, and not on a personal account.

Certificate of deposit (CD)

A certificate of deposit, or CD, is a fixed-rate, time deposit issued by banks and other financial institutions. Upon purchasing the CD, the investor agrees to keep the funds on deposit with the CD issuer for a certain period of time. CDs pay higher interest rates than unrestricted cash deposits. Most CDs are FDIC-insured.

Certified check

A certified check is a draft that's guaranteed by the issuing bank. The bank may set aside the amount of the check from the accountholder's available funds so that the money is not spent before the check is presented for payment. Generally, a bank charges a fee for check certification.

Charitable donation

A charitable donation is a gift of money or property that's given to a nonprofit organization or charity. Many nonprofit organizations rely on charitable donations for continued funding. It's common for taxing authorities like the IRS to provide tax breaks to individuals and commercial entities that make qualifying charitable donations.

Closing costs

These are expenses incurred over and above the price of the property, by buyers and sellers when transferring ownership of property. They are of two types, non recurring and pre paid. The former costs are incurred on items paid just once as a result of buying property or obtaining a loan. Pre-paid are costs which are recurring such as property taxes and homeowners insurance. A lender usually gives the borrower an estimate of the total costs on Good Faith within three days of receiving a home loan application. Closing costs normally include an origination fee, an attorney's fee, taxes, an amount placed in escrow, and charges for obtaining title insurance and a survey. Closing costs percentage will vary according to the area of the country.

Co-signer

A co-signer, or cosigner, is one who agrees to take responsibility for a debt if the borrower defaults. A loan applicant who does not qualify for a loan may be able to obtain financing anyway if he can convince a family member to be a cosigner. The presence of a qualified cosigner makes the loan significantly more attractive to the lender.

Collateral

It is the asset that acts as the guarantee in the repayment of the loan. The borrower may risk losing this asset if he is unable to repay his loan according to the terms of the loan contract or the mortgage or the trust deed.

Compound interest

Compound interest is calculated over the total amount owed, including interest that has accumulated. Borrowers experience compounding interest during negative amortization when the principal amount of the loan actually increases because the monthly payments are lower than the full amount of interest owed.

Consolidation loan

A consolidation loan is a debt facility that pays off and replaces several smaller debts. Debtors would consolidate their debts to lower their monthly payment burden and overall interest rate. Consolidation loans are also called debt consolidation loans.

Consumer Credit Protection Act

The Consumer Credit Protection Act is federal legislation that limits wage garnishments and mandates disclosure of certain terms with respect to credit offerings. The Act was passed in 1968 and is best known for containing the Truth in Lending Act (TILA), which requires creditors to provide consumers with understandable, comparable terms for credit offers.

Contract

An agreement either written or oral, that qualifies whether a certain thing can be done or not.

Contract for deed

The sale of property or real estate in which the buyer takes possession while making payments. The seller holds the title until full payment is made. This may also be called a land contract.

Contractor

The person who constructs or oversees construction of a house or a large renovation.

Conventional Mortgage

This refers to a fixed-rate, 30-year mortgage that is not insured by the government (FHA, Farmers Home Administration (FmHA) or Veterans Administration). In this mortgage the interest rate will not change during the entire term of the loan.

Credit bureau

A credit bureau collects and maintains debt payment histories of individual and corporate borrowers. Lenders use this information to evaluate a prospective borrower's creditworthiness.

Credit card

A credit card is a plastic payment card that's linked to a revolving credit account. The borrower/cardholder uses the card for payment, and receives an itemized statement of transactions at the end of each reporting period. If the balance is not paid in full by the end of the grace period, interest charges are added automatically to the account.

Credit check

A credit check is the review of a loan applicant's debt payment history. Lenders perform this review to predict how the applicant will handle the proposed debt obligations.

Credit history

It is the documented and detailed statement of an individual's fully repaid debts. It helps the lender to ascertain the risk and creditworthiness of a potential borrower and whether he will be able to repay future debts in time.

Credit limit

A credit limit is the maximum amount of debt available to a borrower under a credit card, charge card, or other type of revolving credit facility. The borrower may apply charges to the account only up to the approved credit limit.

Credit report

A documented statement of an individual's credit history and borrower's current credit standing. It is prepared by a credit bureau and used by lenders in determining the creditworthiness of the loan applicant. [www.annualcreditreport.com]

Credit score

A number that reflects the credit history as outlined in that person's credit report. A lender will calculate this number using a computer system as part of the process of assigning interest rates and terms to the loans they make. The higher the number, the better the terms that a lender will offer. A good credit score is around 720. It is possible to raise your credit score over time and by appealing certain items that appear on your report. It is smart for consumers to monitor and track their credit reports to ensure that the information is correct and to make sure that the items that they have disputed do not remain on their reports.

D

Debit card

A debit card is a plastic payment card that's linked to a deposit account. Debit cards are accepted for purchase transactions at participating businesses. When the card is presented and approved for payment, the transaction amount is almost immediately deducted from the account balance. Debit cards can also be used at the ATM for funds withdrawals, deposits, and transfers.

Debt-to-income ratio

Debt-to-income ratio, or DTI, is the quotient of a borrower's minimum debt payments divided by that borrower's gross income for the same time period. DTI is used by lenders as one factor in the evaluation of risk associated with a debt request. From the lender's perspective, a higher ratio indicates greater risk.

Debtor

A debtor is an individual or entity that owes money. Debtors owing money to a bank or lender are called borrowers, and debtors owing money to investors (who have purchased the debtor's bonds or debentures), are called issuers.

Deed

A document or contract of legal bearing with evidence of title to property

Depreciation

A decrease in the value of property or assets. It is used in accounting to show an expense to reduce taxable income. Since it is not an actual expense, only a representation of the decreasing monetary value of a asset in use, lender will add back the depreciation expense for self-employed borrowers and take it as income.

Direct deposit

Direct deposit is an electronic transfer of funds into a bank or credit union account. Direct deposit is most commonly associated with wages; in lieu of paper payroll checks, an employer automatically deposits wages into the employees' personal accounts. The IRS also offers direct deposit of tax refunds.

Discretionary or Disposable income

Discretionary income is the amount of one's earnings that's available for voluntary spending after covering the cost of food, shelter, clothing, taxes, and other essentials.

Diversification

Diversification is a tenet of conservative investing. It calls for spreading out investment funds among different classes of assets, different industries, and/or different companies, in order to reduce risk.

Dividend

A taxable distribution or payment of earnings to shareholders as declared by a company's board of directors. In credit unions, a dividend is the money paid to members for deposits. This is similar to the interest banks pay to their customers for their deposits.

Down payment

The initial and part cash payment towards the price of the property which is not financed by the mortgage.

F

FICO score

FICO score is a numeric value calculated by Fair Isaac Credit Organization that represents creditworthiness. When lenders talk about credit score, they're usually referring to the FICO. FICO is calculated by a secret algorithm that considers an individual's payment history, debt level, and other related factors.

ixed-rate mortgage

A fixed-rate mortgage, or FRM, is a loan secured by real estate property that accrues interest at the same rate throughout the life of the debt.

Foreclosure

It is a repossession of property by a legal process due to default on terms of mortgage by the borrower. This property is sold at a public auction, the proceeds of which are used to settle mortgage debt.

H

HELOC

Acronym for Home Equity Line of Credit

Home equity line of credit

A variation of a home loan, paid as revolving debt that is backed by the portion of the home's value that the borrower owns outright. Interest paid on a home equity line of credit can be used as a deductible. This credit allows the homeowner to write checks against the equity on an ongoing basis to pay for multiple expenses rather than one big sum.

Homeowner's insurance

A policy that includes hazard coverage, loss or damage to property, as well as coverage for personal liability and theft.

Household income

The total income of all members of a household. An important calculation when applying for a joint credit situation

I

Installment contract

A payment agreement in which the buyer makes a series of payments.

Interest

Additional money paid by the borrower for the use of the money, calculated as a percentage of the money borrowed and paid over a specified time.

J

Joint account

A bank account that is owned by two or more persons and who shares in the rights and liabilities of the account.

Joint credit

Credit issued to a couple based on both of their incomes, credit reports, and assets.

Joint liability

When two or more people assume responsibility to repay debt.

Judgment

A legal decision; when requiring debt repayment, a judgment may include a property lien that secures the creditor's claim by providing a collateral source.

L

Late payment fee

A fee charged to the borrower for not making the payment on time.

Lease

An agreement where the property's owner allows a tenant to use the property in exchange for monies for a set amount of time. This may also pertain to an automobile where the borrower uses the vehicle for a set amount of time in exchange for lease payments. At the end of the lease period, the borrower gives the car back to the dealer or arranges to buy the automobile.

Lessee

The person who signs for the lease.

Lessor

The person who is granting a lease.

Liabilities

All of the borrower's debts and legal obligations.

Line of credit

The maximum amount a financial institution is committed to lend to a borrower during a designated time period.

Loan term

The period of time in which the borrower has to repay the loan as specified in the original loan contract. Auto loans are typically 4 years, whereas mortgages have a loan term of 15 or 30 years.

M

Market value

The price that a property is worth based on an agreeable situation between ready buyers and content sellers who have disclosed all the facts about the property.

Millage rate

Millage rate, or mill rate, is a property tax term referring to the amount of tax charged for each dollar of a property's assessed value. The rate is expressed in mills, where one mill equals one-tenth of one cent, or $0.001.

MLS (Multiple Listing Service)

A shared list of information and details on properties that are available in certain areas.

Money market account

An FDIC insured deposit account that allows a maximum of six monthly withdrawals. This allows these accounts to remain liquid and are known as stable accounts because they invest in short term debts with maturities of under a year.

Money market mutual fund

A fund that invests in short term paper debts, designed to produce high yields without the loss of capital.

Mortgage insurance

Insurance that protects the lender from incurring losses against non-payment of home loans. This is required for loans that have an LTV in excess of 80%. When the LTV is more than 80%, the borrower pays higher interest rate to the lender who then pays the premium to the mortgage insurance directly. Certain loan programs like first time home loans are covered by MI irrespective of the LTV percentage.

Mortgage loan

A mortgage loan is a debt instrument that's secured by real estate property. The terms mortgage loan and mortgage are used interchangeably.

Mortgage refinance

The option to pay off an old loan with a new one. This typically saves the borrowers money in terms of a lower interest rate or lower payments. The borrower may also opt to get cash out of his or her equity.

Mutual fund

A mutual fund is a professionally managed portfolio of securities that builds capital by selling shares to investors. Mutual funds give the individual investor access to a diversified, regulated portfolio. The fund publishes its investment strategy and objective along with its historic performance in a prospectus. Gains or losses in the portfolio are shared by the shareholders/investors.

N

Net worth

The total sum of all of your assets minus all debts. Assets include your home, car, investments, etc. Debts include mortgages, credit cards, and loans.

O

Overdraft

Overdraft occurs when drafts or withdrawals exceed an account's available balance of funds. The term is used interchangeably with "insufficient funds." Overdraft can also mean an immediate credit extension, such as when there are insufficient funds in an account and the bank must extend credit to cover pending drafts.

Overdraft protection

Overdraft protection is a service offered on checking accounts. When a customer has it, the banking institution will pay presented checks, even if the funds available in the account aren't sufficient to cover the check amount. There's usually a fee associated with overdraft protection, as well as a per-check fee, when an overdraft situation occurs.

P

Power of attorney

A legal document that authorizes one person to act on behalf of another. There can be a General POA granting compete authority or a specific POA for a specific act or for a certain period of time.

Prime rate

The interest rate that a bank charges its most reliable customers who are the least likely to default on their loan.

Principal

The actual value of a mortgage or note borrowed or the balance left of a loan not taking into account any interest.

Principal, interest, taxes, insurance – PITI

Principal, interest, taxes, insurance, or PITI, are the different parts of a complete mortgage payment. Principal is the amount applied to the debt balance, interest is the monthly accrued financing charges, taxes are pro-rated amounts applied to the annual tax bill, and insurance is the mortgage insurance premium.

Private mortgage insurance (PMI)

It serves to protect lenders against defaults or losses from borrowers. Borrowers are required to carry Private Mortgage Insurance if their loan has loan -to-value percent higher than 80%. Depending on the type of loan the borrower will have to pay an initial premium and a monthly premium.

Property tax

A tax assessed by the state or local government on real estate and personal property whose amount varies depending on the property's value and the various services provided to the property. Property taxes are most often paid into an escrow account and the lender is responsible for paying the taxes when it is due.

Q

Quitclaim deed

The document that transfers the ownership of a title to property and is filed with the government. It often is used among family members and can be used to clear up a gap in the chain of title or inheritance questions.

R

Real property

Unmovable property, like buildings and land.

Roth IRA

A Roth IRA is a type of tax-advantaged retirement savings account available in the U.S. Contributions to a Roth IRA are made with after-tax money, but earnings and qualified withdrawals are tax-free. Qualified withdrawals can't be made until the account has been open for five years and the accountholder reaches aged 59 1/2. Roth IRAs are subject to annual contribution limits and income limitations.

Rule of 72

Rule of 72 is a means of estimating how many years it will take to double an investment that's earning a certain interest rate. To make the calculation, divide the compound interest rate by 72. A 10 percent interest rate, for example, will double an investment in 7.2 years.

S

Savings account

Savings account is a bank or credit union deposit that earns interest and can be withdrawn on demand.

Secured debt

Secured debt is a loan that's supported by collateral. Mortgages are secured, because the lender takes a lien on the property, and has the right to foreclose in a default situation. Auto loans are also secured, because the lender takes a lien on the vehicle.

Simple interest

Interest computed only on the principal balance, without compounding.

T

Tax deferred

Earnings and income that are not taxable now but will be at a later date. This is most common in retirement plans distributions.

Tax exempt

The part of your income that is not taxable or subject to tax.

Tax-sheltered annuity

Tax-sheltered annuity is a type of retirement planning instrument available to employees of tax-exempt organizations. Contributions are tax-deductible and earnings within the annuity aren't taxed until withdrawn.

Treasury bill or Treasury note

Treasury bill, or Treasury note, is short-term debt security that's issued and backed by the U.S. government. Treasury bills are sold at a discount, so that the value of the bond increases as the maturity date approaches. Investors realize yield by purchasing the bond at a discount, and then selling it for a higher price at a later date.

Trust

Similar to a will. A relationship where a person transfers valuables or assets to a trustee who manages this property for the benefit of the beneficiary.

Truth-in-lending act

Disclosure in writing the terms and conditions of mortgage charges and annual percentage rate (APR) as required by the federal law.

U

Unsecured loan

advance of money that is not secured by collateral.

Usury

Illegal and excessive interest.

W

A will is a legally binding document in which an individual specifies how he would like his property distributed after his death. The will can also specify a guardian for dependents and an executor for the estate.

Weight of money

A large amount of money ready to be invested on the stock market, especially cash available in pension funds

The Mission of this Ministry:

"THE WEIGHT OF MONEY"

"a Spiritual Journey"

One **life** at a time, this ministry was birthed with the motivation to help others understand the simple, yet profoundly wise instruction of God's faithful Word. Money will always be a powerful tool for the devil and therefore, a 'distraction' for God's people.

This ministry's mission is to reveal God's heart by revealing the truths of money idolatry in our culture.

To set *free* those lives entangled in the superficial riches of this brief life,
in order to awaken them for the riches to come...
rescue those that don't know the truth ...

because there is a "weight to money" that burdens the souls of the saved and unsaved alike
and yet it is *not* the 'money' itself that causes the angst.

It is the imbalance of man's heart and his motivation
towards money as either a power tool *of giving* or a jack-hammer *of taking*.
we **choose**.

...

Yet, there are scales of a righteous God that gives us a different weight,
A weight worth all the gold and riches afforded,

The Weight of Glory.

The Crown of Salvation and Eternity.

That promises to deliver 'true riches' like no other....

.for *those* who **love their Lord** with *all* of their **mind, heart and soul**.

LA Burning (1992)

Made in the USA
San Bernardino, CA
15 March 2017